At t

GILLIAN CLARKE

At the Source

CARCANET

First published in Great Britain in 2008 by
Carcanet Press Limited
Alliance House
Cross Street
Manchester M2 7AQ

A CIP catalogue record for this book is available from the British Library
ISBN 978 1 85754 986 7

The publisher acknowledges financial assistance from the Arts Council of England

Typeset in Monotype Bembo by XL Publishing Services, Tiverton
Engravings by Thomas Bewick
Printed and bound in England by SRP Ltd, Exeter

Contents

Sgwarnog

'Tell me the names for the hare!'
'*Sgwarnog* for its long ears.
Cochen for its red-brown fur.
Ceinach for its criss-cross course.
Cath y Mynydd, Cath Eithin,
Cat of the mountain, of the gorse.'

There, alive, over the hedge
In the field by the cliff path,
One of her kindle, her young,
A leveret alone stone-still in its cwtsh
Till she comes at dusk to suckle it,
Murmuring mother-tongue.

A Local Habitation and a Name

A Local Habitation and a Name

Houses we've lived in
inhabit us
and history's restless
in the rooms of the mind[1]

Propped on a shelf in the old *beudy* (byre) at Blaen Cwrt is Ordnance Survey Sheet XXXII SW printed in 1953. Today the beudy walls are lined with books, and where the manger used to be, in a corner redolent of hay and the grassy breath of Marged's milking cow, my computer and printer are neatly stowed, as pleasing a design solution as a good metaphor. In Marged's days the wide doorway was open to the wind and the rain, its stone corners rounded to let the cow pass smoothly to her stall. Today, in place of the doorway, a window seat is set below a three-casement window. It looks over rain-washed cobbles that a hundred years ago would be sluiced clean with buckets of well-water veined blue with milk.

The view leads east down a garden that was once yard, stackyard, sty, orchard and kitchen garden, through sycamore and ash trees and an encircling hedge of laburnum. In May we live in a circle of gold. It's said the glorious hedges of *tresi aur*, the golden chain that grows wild round so many fields and along roadsides in this part of Ceredigion, first rooted themselves from fencing stakes peddled by a travelling salesman before the First World War. Beyond the hedge, fields fall to the little river Glowan that flows into the Clettŵr and on into the Teifi, the Irish Sea and the Atlantic. A tributary of the Glowan rises in this garden – source,

---

1 Gillian Clarke, 'Cofiant', *Letting in the Rumour* (Carcanet, 1989).

blaen – to be swollen a field away by Ffynnon y Milgwn. What-
ever hounds met once by the fierce spring named after them it is
impossible to pass it now without hearing their bloody cries. The
stream flows south down a narrow valley in two strands, one either
side of the bank that divides the slopes of Fron Blaen Cwrt from
Allt Maen's steep wood. The strands unite in a froth of shallow
water over stones under the bridge and find a name: the Bwdram,
llymru, source of the word 'flummery': thin beer, a pudding
whisked from leavings; something insubstantial; a nothing.

The land framed by the map was surveyed in 1887, revised in
1904. Set just below the 900-foot contour line, Blaen Cwrt is
marked as a tiny rectangle in the fork of two lanes on the bound-
aries of Fron Felen and Allt Maen. It's a typical Cardiganshire
single-storey longhouse – beudy, barn, two rooms, a *croglofft* (roof
room) reached by a ladder from the larger of the two rooms, and
a dairy. It was built two centuries ago from the stones of the fields,
crammed into the north-west corner of its eighteen acres. It is set
into the high bank under the rising land to the west, its rear wall
hidden by a hedge-bank overgrown with laburnum, rowan and
blackthorn. The two small original windows of the house squint
eastwards, alert for arrows of rain and wind in the suspicious way
of hill farms. Behind, to the west, Allt Ddu rises to a thousand feet.
On rare, ice-clear days, the peaks of Pumlumon, Cader Idris and
Snowdon can be seen to the north from the lane behind the house,
and the long finger of Llŷn almost touching the island of Enlli
(Bardsey) like Michelangelo's Adam reaching for the finger of
God. This is the high land known as Banc Siôn Cwilt, smuggler's
country. In the eighteenth century Siôn, his coat patched like a
quilt (*cwilt*), stowed his contraband in sea caves along the coast six
miles away. Twenty years ago I could have sworn I saw his ghost.
From the cliffs above a small bay called Cwmtydu I watched a boat
with an outboard motor chug ashore. Two men stepped out of a
parked car. There was a transaction, a passing of money. Some-
thing was certainly smuggled.

Other ghosts have left their traces and their names. Some are
benign ghosts whose lost habitations are marked only by the nettles
and gooseberry bushes that show they were ever there: Ysgol Pwll-
y-Pwdel, the old school by the river Glowan; Cae Gwreichion,
the field of sparks where the plough still turns ashes and horseshoes

from the black soil of a long-vanished forge; harp-shaped Cae
Delyn. And Marged, Blaen Cwrt's last long-term inhabitant, who
took her own life one bleak winter in the 1930s; Mamgu, my
grandmother-in-law, walked with Marged past the old school, up
the lane, past Blaen Cwrt and over Allt Ddu to the Capel Cynon
fair a hundred years ago, wearing, she told me on her hundredth
birthday, her best button boots.

The poet Thomas Jacob Thomas, (1873–1945), his bardic name
'Sarnicol' taken from the house a mile away where he was born,
often passed this way, along the 'heol gul garegog', the narrow
stony track – now the B-road from Post Bach – through the farm
yard at Blaen Glowan Fawr. One such morning the yard at Blaen
Cwrt is empty. Where, he wonders, is Bensia, a giant of a man so
strong he could catch a bull by the horns and throw it on its back.
Minutes later he sees no sign of Pegi, Bensia/Benni's grand-
daughter, in the *clos* – yard – at Blaen Cwrt. Was Pegi the young
Marged? He does not see me, either, though I can see him,
through the casement window of my study. Another day he stops
to help Benni Blaen Cwrt break a pile of stones picked from the
fields to sell as hardcore to the roadmakers. Benni advises the poet
to stick to his books so that he won't have to break stones when
he's sixty. Benni's daughter Nani, grieving with 'gweddwdod
anobeithiol',[2] despairing widowhood, is tending the pig in the
yard. She asks the poet when he's going to get a wife.

These things happened here, outside this very window. Still,
sometimes, we dig from the dark soil, along with rusty chains,
horseshoes, fragments of earthenware and the bright, hopeless
splinters of Nani's china, the crescent moon of a pig's jawbone.

A quarter of a mile past Blaen Cwrt the poet descends Rhiw
Amwisg to the crossroads near his birthplace, Sarnicol. Half way
down Rhiw Amwisg is a little quarry full of bluebells in late spring
and rosebay willowherb in summer. You hurry by because it's a
blind bend and the banks are high and steep, because of its name,
Hill of the Shroud, because of restless history, and because they say

2   Thomas Jacob Thomas, 'Sarnicol'.

a man is buried there. Once, on a day of sudden spring, I saw a
glistening cloud of insects on Rhiw Amwisg, airy nothings shaking
out luminous wings in the warmth. The name takes into itself
another defining association: a swarm of sunlight. People tell of a
mysterious highwayman who robbed travellers on that road, the
amwisg a cloak that entirely enveloped him. No one had ever seen
his face, and suspicion fell on a man who suffered a disfiguring and
fatal skin disease. It was never proved. An elderly neighbour, a
'hedge' poet now dead, who lived in a house whose lights we can
see across the valley, used to walk this way. She would stop to talk,
adding a ghost or two to the company of spirits on this hill. She
once told me her grandfather was killed by a highwayman. Her
story too haunts the lanes I walk.

Turn left at the Sarnicol crossroads by the slate plaque engraved
with a few lines of the poet's verse and set in the wall on the cente-
nary of his birth.

A dôf yn ôl i'r dawel fan
O bedwar ban y byd[3]

'To come home to this quiet place /from the four corners of the
world': colliers from the South Wales valleys home for the
weekend; sailors disembarking at Cardiff, Fishguard, Liverpool;
soldiers on the Great Western Railway. Now the exiles come
home on the M4 and the A486, or on a Great Western train from
Paddington.

This lane leads everywhere. It treads unbroken to the horn of
Africa, and crosses eleven time zones to the shores of the Pacific.
It changes its name as it travels. Motorway. Autoroute. Silk Road.
It begins quietly, leading downhill past Allt Maen to the bridge
over the Bwdram where the unseen otter leaves its sprent on the
stones. I leave the lane, climb up through larches to the gorse slopes
where adders lie in summer, through the hanging oak wood where
badgers have built a city, and where, for three weeks in late spring
there will be nothing under the trees or on my mind but the scent

3   *Ar Fanc Siôn Cwilt: Detholiad o Ysgrifau Sarnicol* ('On Fanc Siôn Cwilt: Collec-
    tion of Writings by Sarnicol'), ed. Tysyl Jones (Gomer Press, 1972).

and flooding colour of bluebells. Miles away Llanllwni mountain shines with snow. Far below is wetland, Site of Special Scientific Interest, breeding ground of the Marsh Fritillary butterfly. Down there the pingo hole is blue as sky, a pocket of glacial water left from the last Ice Age 18,000 years ago, now easing again from its cage of ice.

A red kite circles the wood. For a month of frost and stars the barn owl has held us with her cold mythological cry. Now is the kite's turn. His yellow eye burns a point on the land's map until it smoulders in sunlight.

The sheep follow us, hungry. We will bring them hay cut from the fields that Benni, Nani, Marged and their forefathers and foremothers cut before us. We have planted hundreds of trees, restored and planted hedges, levelled a few lumps of their bit of old Wales, made a small lake for dragonflies and swallows, raised a big new barrel-roofed barn for the hay, the tractor, and the coming lambs, and settled into the old house and its linked buildings with our books, music, computers and comforts. Their barn is our bedroom, their dairy part of our big kitchen. The room they called the *parlwr*, with a cupboard bed and loft-ladder, is our *cwtsh*, a cosy winter sitting room. Guests who are young and fit still climb the ladder to sleep in the old croglofft. In the manger corner of their old beudy my words skitter on the screen's ice.

'Mynd at dy lyfre heddi,' 'Stick to your books today,' Benni urges a poet who wants to avoid breaking stones tomorrow,

> And as imagination bodies forth
> The forms of things unknown, the poet's pen
> Turns them to shapes, and gives to airy nothing
> A local habitation and a name.[4]

4 Shakespeare, *A Midsummer Night's Dream.*

Beginning with Bendigeidfran

It seems to have begun with Bendigeidfran, the giant son of Llŷr, King of Britain, brother of Branwen. Calling into the dark cave of language brings his voice echoing back. His story, his rhythmic syllables, the imprint of his huge foot on the shore, and the rocking stone on the headland that was once an apple out of the giant's pocket – these were the first stories located in a geography that was mine.

The sea lies a few hundred yards from the farmhouse door, just a breathless dash down the path, through a kissing gate and over a stile, and a final slide from the shelf of turf, too low to call a cliff, onto the shingle beach. The farm belonged to my grandmother's family from before I was born until I was almost grown up. The path is a sandy track that winds between gorse and over two stiles to a small cove between cliffs that extend parallel arms north-westward into Cardigan Bay. Its black shingle, the grey Atlantic seals that swim in its translucent green waters, the strangely hollowed, footprint-shaped pool in a rock at the foot of cliffs close to the bay, and the story my father taught me to associate with it, have haunted me longer than almost any memory.

According to my father, the giant Bendigeidfran set off in a rage from the beach at Fforest to wade the Irish Sea to rescue his sister Branwen from the Irish court and her sad marriage to the King of Ireland. The stamp of his foot left a giant print in a black slab fallen from the cliffs. Those rocks lie broken on the shore and jut jaggedly from the sea. They still have about them an air of turmoil. Upheaved slabs of black strata from some ancient colliding and pleating of the earth's layers, they loom out of dark times, bringing old tales of war and shipwreck, and bearing messages that seem to be coded or in languages I could not understand.

Seamus Heaney once said that his poetic imagination is rooted in childhood fear. When pressed, he added that every poem he had ever written arose from the sharp, new emotions of childhood. Most poets know that poetry is grounded in the earliest experiences, in memory too deep to name, stored in the senses rather than in the filing-system of the conscious mind. It is upon those feelings and experiences at the wellspring of language, where words are newborn, that the poet needs to draw. No wonder Keats expressed a desire for a life of sensations rather than thoughts. To go back that far is to touch the source, where what is 'real' and what is imagined, what comes from lullaby, nursery rhyme or fairy story, and the white noise of the world that is way over a child's head, on radio, television, in grown-up talk, is all tangled up, unsorted, untouched by understanding or prejudice. It is the pure spring of language. There the human being is brand new. Words store and offer back our memories, and in infancy, when body and mind are single, real and the imagined worlds are indivisible. So there must be a word for it. 'Nothing is until it has a word'.[1]

For me, poetry is a rhythmic way of thinking. It is thought informed by the heart, informed by the body, by the rhythms of breathing, walking, moving. The cadences of poetry are nothing to do with counting syllables. It is breath, pace, gait, gesture. People often ask, does being Welsh influence you as a poet? Or, does being a woman make a difference? I must say yes, it must be, as well, I suppose, as being a whole lot of other things. Writing is informed by the whole self and the whole life lived. Welsh writers in both languages are connected by several common experiences: the relative classlessness of Wales, and the sound of two drums beating. Our placenames and our English speech are haunted by Welsh. We share history, ancestral connections with Nonconformism, farming, heavy industry, and an enduring respect for and ambition for education. There are striking biographical links between the writers of Wales. It is a small country, a place of coincidence and connection.

My parents were, in their different ways, both word people, despite the limited formal education available in their youth. Both

1   Gillian Clarke, 'Llŷr', *Letter from a Far Country* (Carcanet, 1982).

were Welsh-speaking, both from families with their roots and culture in an old, rural Wales, my father from Carmarthenshire, my mother from Denbighshire. My paternal grandfather farmed and worked for the Great Western Railway. His forbears were Baptist ministers, farmers and preachers. My maternal grandfather farmed and milled corn, as had most of my mother's known ancestors. My sister and I were the first members of the family to be brought up with English as mother tongue.

By the time I was born, my father had joined the BBC in Cardiff as an outside broadcast engineer, and my early childhood in that time of war was spent partly in Cardiff, then Barry, and partly at 'home' in Pembrokeshire at the farm to which my widowed grandmother had moved from her native Carmarthenshire. Both my parents valued words, literature, books. Both thought education the way forward for their daughters. My father treasured both his languages, but for my mother the way up and out of hardship was to speak and teach her children English only. A child of a tenant farmer, she noted that her father's landlords were rich, privileged and English, and she made up her mind in bitterness to escape her own heritage. She went to one of those insidiously anti-Welsh grammar schools that destroyed the self-confidence of so many of her generation. She trained as a nurse, and gave it up to marry. Determined that her daughters would be educated, she spoke nothing but English from the day I was born, taught me to read before I went to school, and grudged the sacred place that Welsh held in my father's life. I knew that he spoke it everywhere except at home, so for me Welsh took on the nature of a forbidden tongue, a language of secrets from which I at first felt merely excluded, and later learned to value as something stored away for my future by my father, against my mother's wishes. It is a history very like that of many writers of my generation.

My mother taught me, by endless repetition and song, all the English nursery rhymes. She left the tall tales to my father. Song and story. What gifts could be greater than those? What child could want more?

The myth of Branwen and Bendigeidfran is not traditionally associated with Pembrokeshire. Though the imagination thrills to see and to name the very place, the stones, rivers, caves, islands or mountains as the grave or the birthplace of Branwen, Grainne or Europa, the true geography of myth lies in the mind. My father's version of the tale gave me possession of what was rightly mine, and should belong to all children. It offered me a place in the myth, and gave myth and naming a place in my imagination. By the time I first saw *King Lear* when I was ten, I already knew the tragic story of Branwen/Cordelia, the beautiful daughter of Llŷr/Lear. My first bookcase was full of folk and fairy tale and the mythologies of several cultures, and my head full not only of Enid Blyton but also of the Mabinogion. However, I recall no real book of the latter, no illustrated collection specially for children, only my father's version of the stories told to keep me happy in the car on the frequent journeys between Cardiff and Pembrokeshire, to keep up my pace on a walk, or to get me to sleep at night. In fact the stories kept me awake. I heard the giant Bendigeidfran breathe, cough, stamp and rage in the waterfalls, tides, winds and storms at Fforest, and in the rumours of war on the radio or in the headlines of newspapers. The fact that literature, from nursery rhyme and fairy story onwards, was so closely associated with the natural world, has played a strong part in making me a country person in my head rather than an urban one, even during the years of my life growing up in the city, and bringing up my children there. Literature hallowed the natural with the supernatural. It made the stones sing. It populated the countryside with animals, seen and unseen. It made natural phenomena reverberate with mythological meaning, turned a rocking stone to a giant's apple, a rock pool to a footprint.

Childhood in the 1940s was dominated by a world war which even a child happily evacuated to the loving care of a grandmother, in what still seems like paradise, could not escape. My earliest memories of Fforest Farm coincide with the war years. To a child it was a legendary war, a giant's war of stormy seas, shipwreck, armies that crossed rivers on the body of their commander, bombs that fell from the sky. There was a monstrous enemy leader, and could we but kill him we would all be saved. Bendigeidfran was on our side, but I was not at all convinced that he was a sensible friend. I was not keen on his policy of revenge under those black skies of the early 1940s. Like most children, I found the quarrels of adults painful and bewildering, and what was going on up there and out there was all too raw a re-enactment of the unease in my own parents' marriage, symbolised by their difference over which language they should speak to their daughters. From all this turbulence Fforest was a refuge far safer than a bomb shelter under the stairs in a house in a south Wales port. In my grandmother's house and yard, Welsh and English, birth and death, the real and the imaginary, were all equally natural and elemental and as necessary to each other's definition as the sea is to the land.

That poetry is for me both a creative and a thinking process is illustrated by the very slowness of the thought-journey towards an understanding of these things that has taken place since I began to take poetry seriously in the 1970s. From first publication in *Poetry Wales* in 1971, I began to give poetry due attention, in days of intense work between months of devotion to other things, such as rearing children, and earning a living. At first it was the living moment and its present tense that informed the poetry, and the present was made up in those early days almost entirely of familial matters and domestic relationships, which were the subject of my first book, *The Sundial*.[2] As in school geography, you begin with the self, then explore the local, before you draw a map of the world, the universe. You explore the world in widening circles, deeper understanding. I was curious about my forebears, the women of my past, so in later books I explored the subject of ancestry, first the women's story in *Letter from a Far Country*, then the men's in the sequence 'Cofiant' in *Letting in the Rumour*, in an attempt to find the meaning of the present in the past. Later, among a tangled personal mythology of literature and reality, of real childhood memory and story memory, of legendary and real war, of father country, mother country and the rich turned ground between, new subjects clamoured for attention. They seem objective and external, but they take their source and root from a lived past. All writing is based on experience.

We don't live in the small, quiet worlds of the poets I read at school and university. We live in a big world made intimate by the media and by travel, its grief and beauty brought close. Far

2 Gomer Press, 1984.

away things have moved in to live in our minds and they cannot be ignored. I write in a silent room, in a quiet countryside, on an almost-spring day. If I look up I see fields and hills stretching to the horizon. The radio is off, newspapers unopened, the phone metaphorically off the hook. For hours, days, I can enter the poet's room of silence and privacy. But it can't last, and it is not my role to be reclusive. The ivory castle, and its garret, and our illusions of isolation, were brought to rubble by the wars of the twentieth century, and the winged messengers, bringers of news from those far places. My generation's first journeys were made by radio in the time of war, when wireless 'let in the rumour, grief on the radio'.[3] Insights into the mysterious adult world, awareness of the movements of history as it happened, glimpses of great emotions that would otherwise have been beyond the experience of a child, came as the family listened to news bulletins, and some came from radio drama, especially serialised novels. I associate *Jane Eyre* with winter evenings, my father absent, away at work in the reserved occupation of broadcasting, which exempted him from war service. About thirty years later, when I had become a published poet, came the first real visits to other countries, literary festivals, poetry exchanges with Communist regimes keen to demonstrate their enthusiasm for the arts, and American universities supplementing their creative writing resources with visiting writers from the land of Dylan Thomas.

We were suddenly – it seemed overnight – made aware that the planet could become uninhabitable and that it could die. We all needed a new way to write about the natural world. No longer did it seem right for a poet to pause along the hedgerow to write an Ode to a Primrose. It was an emergency. It was time for a poet to warn. Would Keats, in the light of our knowledge today, have complained about the unweaving of the rainbow? Would he not have found a new nature poetry that praises the way a rainbow is constructed from the seven colours of light split and refracted by a water drop? To combine a curiosity for science with love of the natural world is how humankind must live on earth now, and poetry should speak of it. It is no longer just the concern of those

---

3 Gillian Clarke, 'At One Thousand Feet', *Letting in the Rumour* (Carcanet, 1989).

described as 'nature poets' to protest at the spoliation of the earth, or of scientists to show curiosity and concern for the earth.

Reviews of my first collection, which appeared in 1978, spoke somewhat patronisingly of my concern for domestic issues and the natural world, and I and those who shared my concern were regarded as writing about marginal matters, away from the centre. Many of the writers most concerned with these matters were women, made alert to the danger and worried for the future of an increasingly sick earth by motherhood, and a passionate desire for a good and wholesome tomorrow for their children. It was once seen as nonsense to fear nuclear war. It seems strange now to recall that the notion of the deterrent was popular, in the form of the school cane as well as the bomb. I left education largely in ignorance of science, but I know now that the seeds of excitement about the facts of physics, biology, mathematics, were sown on those westward journeys with my father when, between the stories, he taught me about electricity, gravity, how radio worked, how he sent messages in Morse code during his years at sea as a wireless engineer, where the weather comes from, what stars are. An interest in natural phenomena and the living world arises directly from our night watches for otter or badger, listening for curlew, or spotting a kingfisher, hunting for a rabbit or a trout to supplement wartime rations. New nature poems are scientific rather than lyrical, concerned but not romantic. They aim to match the precision of metaphor and word-patterns to the clarity of the fact. They relish the patterning of things, the connections between the worlds of nature and ideas. They are hard at work redeeming the new jargon and making use of every fresh discovery in search of an imagery to match the times we live in. As Eavan Boland writes in 'The Journey', 'odes on/ the flower of the raw sloe for fever' are all very well, but we must make poems to antibiotics too, lest 'every day the language gets less/ for the task and we are less with the language'. R. S. Thomas, more than any poet I can think of in the English language in Britain, consistently used science and the new nature to warn us of the calamity the earth faced, long before it was fashionable to do so. 'Over the creeds/ And masterpieces', he has said, 'our wheels go'.[4]

4   R.S. Thomas, 'No Answer', *H'm* (Dent, 1972).

We need Bendigeidfran. He is a warning. He embodies the power and strangeness of natural phenomena. He provides us now, as he always has, with the myth we need to explain the world to ourselves. He and Concorde have gone, but their names, meaning and mythology remain, still standing for the connection between things more powerful than ourselves. Giants 'are the metaphors that shift the world':

> Tonight as Concorde folds her tern-wings back
> to take the Atlantic,
> I hear a giant foot stamp twice.
> You can still see the mark he made,
> a black space in the stars.[5]

5   Gillian Clarke, 'Giants', from 'Radio Engineer', 'The King of Britain's Daughter', *The King of Britain's Daughter* (Carcanet, 1993).

Cardiff

War. Radios. The sea. A fox. Stone animals on a castle wall. I can't say what came first, but in an undated long-ago a boy dived from a bridge into black water. It smelt mossy, like a well. My father held me on the parapet while I sent pennies spinning into sunlight before they fell, drowned in tree shadows and the sunless waters of the canal. Brown boys, and boys as white as the marble boys in the museum, jumped into the void hugging their bony knees, and came up blowing water from their noses, sometimes with gold in their fists. Some of my pennies must be down there still, in the feeder canal under Kingsway, dragged by a slap of water or the splash of a rat, deep down under the city where they will never be found.

It was a game for a Saturday morning outing, just me and Daddy. Part of the fun was fear of the drop, the black water, the tunnel, my skin tingling, my heart jumping like a frog. I would put myself to the test, stepping to the edge of any vertiginous darkness before legging it, or hanging there, safe, in my father's arms. The mind's equivalent was 'Who made God?' Tucked up in bed after a story I would ask myself the most frightening question in the world, or allow myself to think about forever and ever until I had to shout for someone to come. According to Ga, my grandmother, I was always asking about God, as her letters to my father and his sisters testify. Once, she writes, I asked her, 'Has God got hands?'

As in reading, or writing, or thinking, it's the risky places that draw me, the deep, the dark, the vertiginous edge, where looking down makes your head spin, and looking up turns the earth. This was the enchanted place, where the canal eeled under Kingsway towards the castle ramparts draped with the gorgeous tails of peacocks, and its wall with the seventeen stone beasts that, according to my father, came to life to prowl the city by night, and where the ghost of Ifor Bach still raised his flag on the tower when Wales were playing England. I wore my new coat with a brown velvet collar, mittens on a string, a hanky in one pocket, my pennies in the other. My father's coat was whiskery tweed and felt like the fur of the black bear in the tobacconist shop near the Prince of Wales Theatre, where, before dirty films and bingo, they showed *Snow White*, or *The Wizard of Oz*, or *Lassie Come Home*.

An outing in the city of tall stories. First, my father's office in the BBC in Park Place, with its tall commissionaires, studios, wires, microphones and mysteries. Then the museum. Later, perhaps, to his favourite cafe in Caroline Street for egg and chips, or down Bute Street to the sailors' pub whose name I forget. Everyone knew him in these places. Sometimes we walked streets with wonderful names: Womanby Street, or Golate where, in the olden days, sailors used to go late to embark on their ships for places I could touch on the globe at home; Westgate Street where, in the future, from a corner of the BBC box at the Arms Park, Cliff Morgan and Onllwyn Brace would become heroes – for me the first of a succession of brilliant partnerships on the field as elusive and dazzling as a pair of hares.

In the museum the Blue Lady's dress is so blue it is a lake of bluebells in Porthkerry woods. So blue that she's the sea off Pembrokeshire. Because of her, blue is my favourite colour. Once I'm seven, I'm allowed to wander the lofty halls, the staircases, the galleries opening out of galleries of this wonderful place all on my own, while my father checks something in his office over the road. In the museum the woman in her Welsh costume cooks *cawl* and Welsh cakes and *bara brith* forever over the red coals of the stove in her lovely old-fashioned farm kitchen. In the museum the fox steps from its den beside a glass stream, one paw raised, its glass eye gleaming.

The museum fox is as real as the fox cub, quivering, hot, with a thrilling smell, that my father carried home in his coat through the bombed streets, all the way home from the office in Park Place. He walked in the dark on broken glass up Cathays Terrace, across the junction of Whitchurch Road where people were running and crying, past the lovely Carnegie Library, the cemetery, the park, the lake, up the hill and all the way to 1 Cyncoed Avenue where, once upon a time, we all lived together: me, my mother, my father, his mother ('Ga', my Mamgu), his sister Doris who was never to be called 'Auntie', her husband Uncle Howard, and my father's eldest sister Ceridwen, known as Ceri, who once tried to run away with a married man, till my father stopped her at Cardiff railway station. 'Worst thing I ever did,' he said time and again throughout Ceri's troubled, single life. Auntie Phyllis, the middle sister, also single all of her long life, Great Western Railway clerk from Carmarthen, self-taught teacher of speech and drama, was a frequent visitor, bringing books and reciting Shakespeare and the Psalms, and telling me not to talk so fast and to watch my enunciation.

I can still feel the quivering heat of the fox cub, but what I see of my father's walk though the bombed city came later from a letter to his mother, my Ga, safe at Fforest, the family farm in Pembrokeshire. The farm was kept going, just, by Jim, the bailiff, and for a while two Italian prisoners of war, Raphael, and Mario, who had motorbikes and let me ride pillion. They were good men. Nazis were bad men. Once, on the A48 near Bridgend, my father pointed to a prisoner being walked on the verge. 'That's Rudolf Hess,' he said. 'A Nazi officer.'

The family came and went between Cyncoed and Fforest like a wandering tribe, Howard between his offices in Cardigan and Windsor Place; my father, travelling the country as O.B. Engineer for BBC Wales. After the night of the broken glass, he took me to Fforest to be safe with Ga by the sea, where the war was just a bad story on the wireless, a winter storm, Bendigeidfran raging at the waves. It was at Fforest in the lawless west that Doris skimmed cream from the tops of the churns in the dairy, and sent me for eggs from hen house and hedge for her delicious cheese sauces; where they laughed, conspiratorial and safe in the farm, to hear that the local policeman called my father 'the whitest man in the black market' for supplying his friends at home with contraband eggs and ham – imported to Cardiff once, they said, in a hearse, and where my uncle was fined for 'watering the milk'. I don't think they did water the milk. It was just that Doris too frequently skimmed the churns to make her marvellous dishes of field mushrooms and cream on toast, and the best cauliflower cheese in the world.

I can't date or explain it, but once, earlier, 1940 or so, my father carried me up the gangplank onto a ship in Cardiff docks. My glamorous mother followed. ('She was so pretty she took our breath away,' the chemist in Cyncoed told me years later.) She wore high heels. It was night. We climbed down steep steps into the ship's belly. A beautiful man met us. He was the Belgian captain, my father's friend from the days when he was a ship's wireless officer for the Marconi company before he met my mother and joined the BBC. The captain gave us a mango. The juice ran down my chin. The sea lapped at the porthole. The cabin rocked. When I woke up I was in bed at home and thought I'd been dreaming, except that next day I watched my mother plant the big mango stone in a pot. A beautiful stone, like the keel of a little ship, draped with the golden fibres of the fruit. It never grew.

Our house in Cyncoed had been 'the first house on the meadow'. An elderly neighbour told me so when, years later, at twenty-two, newly married, I returned there to live in the upstairs flat. No other house has established itself in such detail in my mind. I lived there at crucial periods of my life, times when heightened awareness of the indoorscape lays down rich memories: earliest childhood, the first years of marriage, the birth and upbringing of three children. Other places left the outdoors more strongly printed on my mind – Fforest, especially, where rocks, sea and cliffs, woods and waterfall, shippon and hayloft are clear and detailed, while the farmhouse interior remains vague. Number 1 Cyncoed Avenue was familiar in the complete meaning of that word, a house I can never leave behind. In my poem-sequence 'Cofiant' ('Biography') I say:

> Houses we've lived in
> inhabit us
> and history's restless
> in the rooms of the mind.

It works both ways. I can enter that house right now, because it is a part of me:

> How can you leave a house?
> Do they know, who live there,

how I tread the loose tile in the hall,
feel for the light the wrong side of the door,
add my prints to their prints to my old prints
on the finger-plate?

How, at this very second,
I am crossing the room?

I still recall, learning to walk on the oak parquet hall floor, the
pleasing rattle of the few loosened blocks under my feet. We lived
downstairs with Ga. Doris and Howard, and sometimes Ceri, lived
upstairs. When Doris and Ceri quarrelled, Ceri would rant and
wail and depart in a huff to live in a caravan in somebody's field.
As the house resettled into itself, the consensus was, 'Good
riddance'. She was always welcomed home after a month or so.

As a baby I lived mostly in the garden in a black pram with a
white silk fringe on the hood. Trees trembled over my pram. I
know now they were poplars. Their roots reached under the clay,
shrinking and surging with the weather, cracking the walls of the
family house they had built for £700. Uncle Howard was an archi-
tect. He did well. He built the Art Deco Plaza Cinema, and the
bowling club with the undulating roof that collapsed in a great
snow in the 1980s, and eventually his own house in Sherbourne
Avenue, whose interior, even as a child, I loved. I suppose it
must have cut a dash at that time, a modern house in a suburb of
traditional dwellings. It was stylish, all blond wood and pastels like
the colours in Art Deco cinemas, ivory, apple green and old rose
sharpened with dashes of black, and a white baby grand piano that
nobody played.

It was Doris and Howard, the rich aunt and uncle, who intro-
duced me to the theatre, the footlights, the opening chords of the
orchestra, the swishing sigh as the great curtain rose or fell. Every
Boxing Day they took a box at the New Theatre for a family trip
to the pantomime. My sister and I wore party frocks for the occa-
sion.

My mother, who aspired to education's privileges, yearning for
them with a hopeless air of personal disappointment, handed me
a mixed bag of gifts and deprivations. She taught me to read before
I went to school, but she banned Welsh. Her own experience as

one of ten children of a Welsh-speaking family demonstrated that a tenant farmer's Welsh-speaking children were poor, while a landlord's English-speaking family were rich. 'I want you to get on in the world,' she said. According to her the South Wales in-laws laughed at her North Wales Welsh. Maybe, but life had made her over-sensitive, and vulnerable to the South Wales humour. She sang me nursery rhymes, taught me wild flower names, let me stay up late to listen to *Saturday Night Theatre* on the radio, and *Jane Eyre* serialised on Friday nights, and planned the doubtful blessings of elocution lessons and boarding school if I didn't shape up. My father set the stories of the Mabinogi in locations wherever we happened to be – in Fforest, in Cyncoed, in Kingsway, in Roath Park. He took me to the Arms Park, and the opera. First, *The Magic Flute*, in one of the theatres and cinemas that used to rank Queen Street. Auntie Phyllis, the railway clerk, took me to *Peter Pan* in the New Theatre, and got me a week off school every year to visit Stratford. My first Shakespeare play was *King Lear*. I was ten, and wept for the old man who broke friends with his daughter.

One day the family story would fall into place, the 'real' become distinguished from the myth. I eavesdropped on grown-up talk in Welsh and English: voices rattling away above my head in a seethe of rumour, gossip, quarrels, scandal, malice, stories, the Bible, Grimm, Hans Anderson, the Kathleen Fiddler Omnibus; my father's stories on the slow road between Cardiff and Pembrokeshire as the danger of bombs came and went. Words. Delicious words. Names. Coed ar hyd y Glyn. Splott. Golate. Brains Dark. Coedpoeth up north where Nain and Taid lived, and Gobowen, and Wrexham Lager Beer. Once at Fforest, balancing on the slippery wall that dammed the flow of slurry between the shippon and the sloping yard, I was muttering favourite words, collected into a couplet, stamping its beat as I went:

> Ga puts mentholatum on her sciatica
> And Ceri soaks the clothes in Parazone.

Parazone. I fell. Ga called my name. Someone pulled me out and carried me squirming like a piglet to the pool under the waterfall where clean little shadows of freckled brown trout darted away as I was plunged, shouting, in icy water. They carried me home, rinsed of muck, to be bathed by Ga in the scullery sink and dried by the fire to wait for Daddy to come and hear the sorry tale.

We moved from Cyncoed to Barry. Ga came too. 'Flatholm', Lakeside, Barry, our own house overlooking Cold Knap Lake. It was a white house with a flat roof and bay windows that followed the curve of its prow like a ship, and a flagpole where my father ran up the Y Ddraig Goch (the Welsh Dragon) to flutter in the wind off the Bristol Channel as if we were, indeed, aboard ship. Doris said the house was the height of style. Both my parents had left school at fourteen, Llanelli Grammar School and Grove Park Grammar School, Wrexham, respectively, The only surviving son and youngest child of a rural railwayman, and the tenant farmer's daughter who became a nurse, where did they get such ideas, and aspirations to have what they could not afford? I knew they couldn't afford it. Doris said so. I worried.

Soon after that I had a sister, four and a half years younger than me, enough to give us separate childhoods. Eat your egg, there's a war on. Bombs fell on the docks. A piece of shrapnel made a hole in our dining room window. A German shell hit a ship with a cargo of oranges at Barry Docks, and broken crates littered the shore of the Little Harbour. Trained early to forage in food-rationing days, we children staggered home with our jumpers, skirts and knickers filled with fruit, the first real oranges we'd ever seen. One night my father woke me and took me to the window of my bedroom over the porch to see the lights of hundreds of planes flying over-head. 'Look!' he said. I looked. I listened. The roar of so many planes and the dazzle of so many lights. ' I want to you to see this. Never forget it. It's a moment of history.' It would be sixty years before I understood what we saw that night in the sky over Barry, as those planes flew south over the Bristol Channel. It was just before D-Day, and my father, with his ear to the wires at the BBC, knew something was afoot.

And, in Llandough Hospital, Ga died, my last sight of her in her blue dressing gown, blowing kisses from a high window.

They sold Flatholm, 'because of money,' said Doris, and after months in lodgings in Felden, The Parade, we moved to Penarth, first to Cwrt-y-vil Road, and soon to Oaklands in Plymouth Road – a considerable up-sizing of our quarters. It was a large Victorian house in half an acre of garden, 'Cheap,' my mother said, 'because it wants lots doing to it.' The plan was that my mother would turn the house into a guest house, and I would go away to school. From the start I loved that house, the big square rooms, the secret corners, the oak floors and turn of the century stained glass, the large walled garden, ruined greenhouses, old coach house and stables, and the v-shaped glimpse of the sea from my bedroom window at the top of the house. Years later I learned that Oaklands had once been the home of the painter Ray Howard-Jones who so perfectly recorded the wild Pembrokeshire coast I knew. My father spent his every spare minute keeping it from falling apart.

We could always see the sea, from wherever we lived: distantly from the house in Cyncoed, just a few hundred yards away at Fforest Farm, and from Flatholm, and between roof-tops from my attic bedroom in Plymouth Road. From my bed in Cyncoed I lay in the dark listening to thumps and clangs from the steelworks and trains going east, and a colony of tawny owls in the woods and fields that would become the Llanedeyrn estate, where a woman was murdered while out blackberrying. The murder was never solved. She and her basket of fruit still haunt those acres that look east over the Rhymney. From my cot in Flatholm I heard planes from the air base at St Athan, and RAF men rolling home after Saturday dances at Bindles. In Penarth the call of the Breaksea lightship on a foggy night most moved me, one long moan before its voice broke. Then again.

And always the sea. Voices off. Rows downstairs. And radios. Wireless sets, they used to call them. Behind glass in the lit cave of each of our many radios was a needle, and with that needle you could navigate the world just by turning the knob. Later, on the bridge of a ship, holding the wheel tight, trying to keep the needle on a steady course, I remembered those first voyages by radio through the languages, the crackling wastes of ocean between Cardiff, Athlone, Hilversum, Moscow, and home to *Children's Hour.*

Nothing could put me off the sea, or water, even that early baptism of body and soul under the waterfall. I had to be hauled out of swimming pools by attendants, and called from the sea by Ga or my parents. Cold Knap Baths, Penarth Baths, the sea at

Fforest. Even the lost boy didn't stop me, though his ghost haunts
every narrow place where the sea sucks or where water flows
underground. The cover came off an exit pipe at Cold Knap Lido,
and a boy was drawn into the pipe, where he drowned. And turned
to marble. A boy called into the mountain by the Pied Piper. A
girl from my class at Romily Road Junior School, Barry, a
Traveller's child from the caravans, was taken and murdered.
Somewhere else two other children were found half buried in
leaves in a wood. *The Mirror*, or *The Graphic*, or *The News of the
World*, headlined the story 'Babes in the Wood'. My mother hid
the paper but I saw it. Story became life, life became story. It
happened far away, but for me it was Porthkerry Woods, with
bluebells and the sound of the sea, a train crossing the viaduct and
my feet running down dry woodland paths and out over pebbles
in broad sunlight where my mother was unpacking the picnic.

Stories layered with stories, all laid down in the mind to become
part of being.

It's often said, and it's true: children were free then as they are not
free now. At the age of eight or nine we'd leave home after break-
fast and not be expected home till dusk. We (my friends and I)
walked along the beach from Barry to Porthkerry. We made fires.
We built dens in the wild wood between the park and school. We
got deliberately marooned on Sully Island – a peninsula when the
tide is out, but an island at high tide. At ten or eleven years old, I
and a friend would cycle from Penarth to Cardiff, under the
subway from Penarth Dock to Ferry Road, then up through
Grangetown, the castle grounds and on to Rhiwbina woods, or
over the mountain to Caerphilly. We caught trains to unplanned
destinations. Best of all, I would wait at the end of the pier in
Penarth, alone or with a companion, for a Campbell's steamer
bound for Weston or Ilfracombe. At dawn, with a queue of other
voyagers, leaving my bike chained to the pier, I would wait for the
boat to hove into view. *Glenusk, Glengower, Ravenswood* or *The
Bristol Queen,* or, best of all, *The Cardiff Queen.*

     When, at eleven, I went to boarding school in Porthcawl,
another of my parents' unaffordable aspirations, for seven years
Cardiff became The Weekend and The Holidays. Weekends we'd

go shopping, my mother, my sister and I, in the big city stores. My mother was always entranced by the glow and glamour of department stores, Howells and David Morgans and Evan Roberts. While she bought fish at the still-famous stall in the covered market, I'd slip upstairs to see puppies in the pet stall, and browse in secondhand books finding, once, a copy of *The Maid of Sker*. I wanted to read it because of *Lorna Doone,* and because it had local places in it – Newton, Sker House, and Tusker Rock.

Then we'd go with our treasures to have tea in the Angel or the Royal, fingering the papery packages, sniffing our wrists for free perfume trials, looking at a Vogue dress pattern, a bolt of floral cotton, items from Haberdashery or Lingerie – Oh the words! – reading *Woman's Own* and *School Friend* over tea and cakes. I'd have a new school blouse from Roberts, maybe a library book, some romance I hid from my mother – *The Sheikh*, or something by Ethel M. Dell, and Dickens. There was no such thing as teenage fiction, and no transitional literature between childhood and adulthood.

Libraries had always been full of objects of desire. To a bookworm, there is nothing so bleak as reaching the last word of the last page of a book an hour before bedtime, and nothing more thrilling than the Saturday morning find in the library, a new novel by a favourite writer, or something vaguely illicit, and hours of secret reading ahead. It was almost a vice. From early childhood I'd read all night, unable to stop turning pages. In school I read under the blankets by torchlight. Home for the holidays, sent to make the guests' beds in the roomy old house in Plymouth Road, I'd be caught out reading the books on the bedside tables.

One weekend, home from school, at Doris and Howard's in Sherbourne Avenue, I staged my first political demonstration. First to have a television, they invited us all to watch the Coronation. I sat on the window seat, 'nose in a book', while my mother complained that I was 'missing history'. I declared myself a Republican. When I did sneak a look, I saw a grainy grey picture, the white face of the new Queen lost in the rain.

In my O-level year, my father fell seriously ill. After an operation, he took six months recuperation leave from the BBC, and went to Patagonia as a supernumerary on a banana boat. While he was away, and I was mostly at school, something changed in my mother. Her disappointment at his lack of promotion into management in the BBC had embittered her. He came home for Christmas looking tanned and well, but it was a bleak season. I saw that he was estranged in his own home. He had brought home recordings he had made among the Welsh-speaking people of Patagonia, talking, and singing in their *eisteddfod*. The BBC refused to use the tapes because my father was an engineer, not a programme maker. I sensed his, and her deepening disillusion. Forty years later, in the museum bookshop, I looked up my father's name in the index of John Davies's *Broadcasting and the BBC in Wales*. Writing about the BBC's prejudice against its own Welsh-speaking staff, John Davies quotes their treatment of my father as an example of the way being a Welsh speaker could actually be a disadvantage: 'J.P.K. Williams, appointed assistant maintenance engineer at Cardiff in 1928, was denied promotion because the superintendent engineer "did not consider that the Welsh temperament (was) as suited to supervisory duties as the English temperament".'

I was standing in the lofty foyer of the museum, which I'd loved all my life. My father had been dead thirty-seven years. I felt a bomb go off in my mind. My mother's bitterness was justified. These bigots had blighted our lives.

We five 6th formers were St Clares Convent's first university entrants. My father was ill again. Money had run out. My sister was away at school. Instead of going away from home to study I went to Cardiff University on a county scholarship, and travelled daily from Penarth.

I was in love with the very idea of university, and relished my new life. Cardiff was suddenly glamorous. Home from boarding school, I was grown up, an undergraduate. I loved the Civic Centre, the ornate white buildings, the rose-red road of Edward VII Avenue where I walked to college every day under huge elms that touched overhead. Later, they all died, every one, of Dutch Elm Disease. I saw them felled. It was like watching a great cathedral fall.

On my first day as an undergraduate I walked from the station up Westgate Street, Castle Street, Kingsway, under the cloudy elms of Edward VII Avenue, through the Gorsedd Gardens, up the crescent of the drive, under the portico and into the cool and lofty spaces of the university building, excited, and terrified that now I'd arrived I would have to speak to someone.

Just being in the library with an essay to write, books spread on the table, the sentences shaping themselves, made me feel I was on my way. By day, when I wasn't at lectures, or lounging with new friends in the women's common room, in the Students' Union or the Kardomah, I liked to stay on in the city as long as possible. If I went home there'd be housework to do, my father to worry about. I'd be back to my old life. So I'd work on in the lovely university library in Old College, whose generous space barbarians would later destroy with an ugly mezzanine floor. In the evening, after a cup and a scone at the Hayes Island Snack Bar, where tea was poured into ranked cups on a battered aluminium tray in a continuous hit-and-miss stream, I worked upstairs in the old Central Library, where a tramp snored over a book he wasn't reading and pigeons cooed on the window ledges – sounds I still associate with books, with reading, with falling in love with the idea of study, and with English Literature. In the same way, sitting annual exams became associated with the banners, bands and choirs of the Miners Gala passing down Queen Street on a hot June day.

Was I really working? I put the hours in, certainly, and got a kick out of writing a good essay, all the while wired to the presence of male undergraduates – the ratio was four men to one girl in those days. The library stairs were good for swirling a circular skirt with a then-fashionable flicker of broderie anglaise beneath, the table in the alcove perfect for hoping, under the guise of studiousness, that the student at the next table might be looking your way.

Learning for learning's sake would, we were told, give us the world. This seems amazing now. I don't think many students feel the romance of university that we did. We knew we were privileged and were grateful for it. I was no scholar, but I loved English, language excited me, and reading gave me other worlds. My fellow undergraduates were mainly from the mining Valleys, colliers' children, all of us backed by whole tribes of relatives, all excited to be pioneers, to be young, to be the generation given the big chance. We were the granddaughters of the Suffragettes, the children of Nye Bevan and the Welfare State. We were political. We voted. We marched. We demonstrated. I listened, dazzled, to Michael Foot speak passionately and brilliantly in Crwys Road Chapel. It was obligatory to wear academic gowns to lectures and in town, so we were a conspicuous group. Cardiff belonged to us. The places where we consorted, flirted, romanced, sorted the world out, planned the anti-Suez march, anti-war or anti-nuclear demonstrations – the Students' Union, the Kardomah, the Hayes Island Snack bar, the pubs, the Old Arcade, the 'Woody' – put a new, grown-up Cardiff under my skin and into my bloodstream.

May, in my second year, my father died in a nursing home on Penylan Hill. His last words to me were, 'Hwyl fawr, fach.'[1] All the bigwigs of the BBC attended his funeral.

I graduated, got a job in the BBC in London, and after eighteen months of being a stranger with a funny accent, I came home to Wales for good to marry my boyfriend from university days, and to live in 1 Cyncoed Avenue again. Our children were born there. We remained married for ten years, and then, not surprisingly, found we were not who we'd been at eighteen and twenty-one respectively, and we grew in different directions, while remaining friends, remaining family.

In the 1990s we sold the house in Cyncoed, the house my mother had brought me home to when I was days old. Selling up was a painful moment, and a moment of freedom. We sold a house and an attic of skeletons. I cut ties, and shed a lot of luggage. My daughter and sons, all born to that house, two in my parents' old bedroom, had grown up and left home for art college and university. My life had shifted west to my ancestors' country, to a new life. I went home to the house where I was born less and less in the last years. I'd found it was possible to live somewhere else, without ever leaving the city in my bones. I kept what I wanted, left the rest in the skip in the road.

It's my daughter's city now, and her children's. The new Café Quarter is a step from the market, the Hayes Island Snack Bar. There is a new hum of confidence, and somewhere called Cardiff

---

1 'Goodbye, darling.'

Bay that we called 'down the Docks'. But listen to the voices, the gossip, the nosiness, the unstoppable cheek and humour, the interrogation of strangers. Take a taxi. 'Where d'you live? West Wales? There's lovely. Got a caravan in Tresaith. Small world.' We are driving past the castle towards Kingsway. I ask, 'Which is your favourite animal, on the wall?' 'I likes the bear.' 'Me too!'

Cordelia's 'Nothing'

Where do poems come from? An architect sees an interior before he sees the building. Before a roof and walls there is space and light. That's how it feels when a poem is about to form: there is an idea, an image, a fuzzy line, a fizzing excitement, but the words have yet to speak. Even if there are words it is somehow too dark to read them, though a phrase or a line may be legible already. But as soon as this unclear vision declares its presence one can be certain that the poem can be written.

For me, the poem arrives in a coinciding moment of language and energy. Its subject is like a novelist's plot – merely an excuse to rummage in the mind for language. There are few plots and all writers share the same small store, using them over and over again. When a poem is on the way it feels as though energy has been lying in wait for language. Or is it the other way about? And whence does that language come flooding, as strongly as any of the driving human passions, and as suddenly, as mysteriously? The poem is begun in that moment of germination, though it must be unmade and made again in the cold light of the mind before it can be called a finished work of art. To have an *idea* for a poem is to have nothing at all.

In 1990, at the first of the Hay-on-Wye Literary Festival weekend 'Squantums', the plot offered to six poets late on Friday evening was 'Border: Fatherland, Motherland'. What I saw at once was that border country in the self where mother and father meet, an edge where there is both tension and conflict. At the same time it was the border where the two languages of Wales define themselves and each other, and the definition of self and the other was one of the most intriguing aspects of the subject. The meaning of border deepened, layer by layer. I saw those borders inside Wales like a backwards journey into history where the post-industrial south dwindles among tin sheds and tethered alsatians, where sad ponies starve on the yellowed grass of slag, and where, one ridge onwards, another Wales begins as a mountain tilts westward into pasture and wooded valleys. Somewhere in this complex mental landscape of fractures and sutures a childhood tilts into adulthood. The poem I want to discuss was prompted by that moment. But before I can arrive at that poem, I should return to the place whence I think it came, and try to chart its long progress.

The Irish Sea breaks on the shores of my father's land of Dyfed,[1] specifically a small stretch of north Pembrokeshire. We are walking the beach. My father is a great storyteller, and today he tells me the story of Branwen and the giant Bendigeidfran, the children of Llŷr, explaining to his young daughter, mythologically, historically and geologically, two features of the coast close to my grand-mother's farm, known as Fforest. One is a vast rocking stone, or logan stone, probably Neolithic, balanced on the cliff and visible from the farmhouse. It is the giant's apple, or sometimes his pebble, as the story is ever-changing. The other is the black rock-pool vaguely the shape of a footprint and as big as a bath, which fills with sea water at high tide. It is, my father tells me, a footprint burnt into the shore by the enraged Bendigeidfran, setting off for Ireland to rescue Branwen from her cruel life as the rejected wife of the Irish king.

As a child I used to play a game which I called 'big and little', which now seems to me a primitive version of a poet's game, physical and imaginative in nature, yet a child's way into a questioning habit of thought. Half-close your eyes and stare, or blur your ears. A stone becomes a planet. Your breath is the wind, a quarrel is a storm, a storm becomes a war. It works the other way too. Your cupped hand can balance the pebble of the setting sun before it is dropped into the sea. With a finger you can blot out a Neolithic stone, or a planet. Take a magnifying glass to your thumb-print. Place a hair under a microscope. These are geographies. It is a game played with scale and perspective that has always fascinated me. It

1 Dyfed, the name of the ancient princedom, was until recently used for the south-west counties of Wales, including Carmarthenshire, Pembrokeshire and Ceredigion.

prepared me for the theory, later encountered when I began to study Shakespeare, of man as microcosm, the epitome of the macrocosmic universe.

A poem can be a long time coming. Mine often send signals decades before they arrive. I first 'studied' Shakespeare seriously at school for A-level but by then I had often been taken to the theatre and was sufficiently familiar with more than a dozen of the plays to find the characters and their language entering my dreams. I knew passages by heart. I had Lawrence Olivier's autograph. I had seen his spittle glitter on the air when, as Titus Andronicus, he hissed 'because I have no more tears to shed' in a whisper that carried to every ear in the house. Theatre was the most glamorous source of stories that I knew.

Of all the plays it was *King Lear* which first and most powerfully touched the fiction of my own inner life. At ten years old I was taken to see the play at Stratford-on-Avon by one of my father's three sisters, an aunt who was no scholar, merely a railway clerk with a love of books. Soon afterwards she took me to *The Tempest*. They seemed familiar dramas, these father and daughter plays set in a damp Atlantic Ocean past in which I felt I stood and walked and spoke, and had my own part to play. In a recurring dream of childhood I'm walking by the sea and someone is whispering, 'The isle is full of noises'.

From my infancy Europe had been at war, and the theatre of war, as far as I could understand it, was the radio. Because of my father's job there were radios in every room. The radio on the ocean-facing windowsill at Fforest was a teller of wild tales that came straight off the Irish Sea, as did the rain and the wind and the refracted light of the setting sun. These were stories of a great enemy who must be killed so that we could all be safe again. My father's radio was the voice of the story-teller. Later, when I was ten, I was to hear Shakespeare's words, and would at once know they were describing the 'sounds and sweet airs' of Fforest. It was not difficult to imagine my grandmother's farm as an isle full of noises, cut off by the sea, poor roads, weather and the family from bombs, sirens and air raids, though not from the rumours of war. Life into language equals fiction.

It was that complex experience of real life tangled with the life of the imagination that lay in wait for the language I was to hear that first time at the Memorial Theatre, Stratford. To two connecting stories I already knew – the story of Branwen, and my own – was added the story of Lear, which came in words so awesomely mysterious that I was to remember fragments of it forever. It would enter the ground of my mind, along with hymns, and passages of the King James translation of the Bible regularly repeated just as theatrically in chapel. I was an early reader, and I entered books at an age when it is natural to confuse the real world with the world of literature, the self with the characters in stories. Thus, alongside nursery rhymes, 'the moon doth shine as bright as day', or 'the man in the wilderness said to me', playground games, 'Poor Mary is a-weeping', biblical language such as 'tell it not in Gath, publish it not on the streets of Escalon', and the great Welsh hymns, 'Dyma cariad fel y moroedd', 'Here is love like the sea', or the hauntingly simple poetry of 'There is a green hill far away', came the equally strange and beguiling spells of Shakespeare, spells such as 'Nothing will come of nothing. Speak again'. I have not, nor will I check these quotations from the Bible, the hymn book, and from Shakespeare. This is how I remember them. This is how the words must stay, even, perhaps, in misquotation. Those words, in that order, are a part of the 'fiction' I have been writing all my life.

The earliest poem-harbinger of 'The King of Britain's Daughter', as far as I can see, was a poem called 'Llŷr', written around 1980. It was commissioned by the late Sam Wanamaker for one of his series of anthologies, *Poems for Shakespeare*. 'Llŷr' recalls the earliest ecstatic moment of my own experience of Shakespeare's spellbinding power. It carries hints that, like many children, I was in thrall to language, from the first lullaby, the first nursery rhyme, the first hymn, the first playground chant. Llŷr, King of Britain, is Lear, and my father, and he will later hand on his role in my mind to his son, Bendigeidfran (the brother I never had), or Brân, to give him his shorter name. There is no hint of that story in the poem 'Llŷr'. I am Cordelia, and if Cordelia is the daughter of Llŷr, she must also be Branwen. So it was that, without knowing it at the outset, I embarked on the ambitious project of a long poem about childhood in a time of war, with the Bible, the Mabinogion, the Complete Works of Shakespeare, and a book of nursery rhymes in hand.

In the poem 'Llŷr', precursor of the later sequence, I use the land-
scape of Llŷn in Gwynedd, where I happened to be staying when
I wrote it:

> Ten years old, at my first Stratford play:
> The river and the king with their Welsh names
> Bore in the darkness of a summer night
> Through interval and act and interval.
> Swans moved double through glossy water
> Gleaming with imponderable meanings.
> Was it Gielgud on that occasion?
> Or ample Laughton, crazily white-gowned,
> Pillowed in wheatsheaves on a wooden cart,
> Who taught the significance of little words?
> All. Nothing. Fond. Ingratitude. Words
> To keep me scared, awake at night. That old
> Man's vanity and a daughter's 'Nothing',
> Ran like a nursery rhythm in my head.

It is no accident that I chose the fourteen-line stanza and, more or
less, iambic pentameter. The formal use of capitals initialling each
line now looks old-fashioned to me. I abandoned a stiffer earlier
draft using regular rhyme, though the chiming within the poem is
important to it, and deliberate.

The remembered performance by Charles Laughton is substan-
tiated by others, and I believe it to be the one which mainly
influenced the description in Leon Garfield's 'King Lear' in his
version of Shakespeare's stories:

> a mad, wild old man, stuck all over with wild flowers, and
> crowned with weeds

and later,

> Gentle hands had taken him, and tended him, and washed him,
> and put him in fine soft clothes.[2]

---

2 Leon Garfield, *Shakespeare Stories* (Puffin Books, 1997).

The evidence of obsessions that would later be developed in 'The King of Britain's Daughter' can be drawn from hints that lie in the poem 'Llŷr': 'the significance of little words', the list of the words which Shakespeare plays with in the drama, and

> a daughter's 'Nothing',
> Ran like a nursery rhythm in my head.

Rereading the next stanza now, I am surprised and pleased to see the image of the bruise in the sea, a metaphor which, by the time I wrote 'The King of Britain's Daughter', I had forgotten I had used before. I see no reason to avoid repeating the natural and instinctive use of such an image, since it is the thread of unity holding poem to poem, book to book. In 'Llŷr' the description of the height of the cliffs comes from Shakespeare, as well as from personal observation, looking down at the sea from the cliffs of Llŷn:

> I watch how Edgar's crows and choughs still measure
> How high cliffs are, how thrown stones fall
> Into history, how deeply the bruise
> Spreads in the sea where the wave has broken.

Shakespeare puts it this way:

> How fearful
> And dizzy 'tis to cast one's eyes so low!
> The crows and choughs that wing the midway air
> Show scarce so gross as beetles,

and fifteen years after 'Llŷr' I wrote, in 'The King of Britain's Daughter',

> On the headland is an absence
> where it fell some winter night
> between here and childhood,
> and the sea's still fizzing
> over a bruise that will not heal.

Although the cliffs I experienced as a child were real cliffs, it was
when the experience met the language of Shakespeare that I knew
how to feel their height. It was the language of poetry that turned
the dizzy view from a cliff-top into a whole experience, from a
vertigo of the body into a vertigo of the mind and the imagina-
tion. 'Llŷr' links other aspects of the Lear memory with the future
King of Britain poem: 'figures of old men', 'the bearded sea', and
'guilty daughters'. The last verse submits to an irregular, perhaps
an eccentric rhyme scheme:

> Night falls on Llŷn, on forefathers,
> Old Celtic kings and the more recent dead,
> Those we are still guilty about, flowers
> Fade in jam jars on their graves; renewed
> Refusals are heavy on our minds.
> My head is full of sound, remembered speech,
> Syllables, ideas just out of reach;
> The close, looped sound of curlew and the far
> Subsidiary roar, cadences shaped
> By the long coast of the peninsula,
> The continuous pentameter of the sea.
> When I was ten a fool and a king sang
> Rhymes about sorrow, and there I heard
> That nothing is until it has a word.

That 'nothing', unconsciously stolen from Shakespeare, has
become, I suppose, the absence on the cliff, the fallen stone, the
father who died, which I will explain when I discuss 'The King of
Britain's Daughter'.

The storm in *Lear* is almost one of the characters in the play.
Weather is a ready metaphor, and winters in Pembrokeshire hurled
the great Atlantic at the windows of Fforest Farm. Downstairs,
family life simmered in a *cawl* comprising, in various combinations
at different times, a large cast of characters coming and going about
the constant figure of my grandmother. Those exits and entrances
were of my father, mother, sister, three aunts, an uncle, and several
surrogate uncles who were farm workers. I think of the ash tree
lashing the windows in a poem by D.H. Lawrence where down-
stairs his parents are quarrelling. Not only adult rows, but the

babble of downstairs after a child's bedtime, the imperfectly tuned disharmonies of radio, talk, dispute, hint and rumour, send upstairs to the listening child a message that the world is full of tumultuous secrets. Legends made sense of the rumours, as was, I believe, their original function, when the earliest storytellers made metaphors of human history and psychology in the light of man's understanding of the world at the time. Both our childhood selves and our ancestral selves might quite logically see war as a giant, for instance.

Staying at the Smithy, Llanthony, owned in the early nineteenth century by the poet Walter Savage Landor, on the first day of the Hay-on-Wye weekend in June 1990, I began work on my commission. I wrote a poem under the working title 'The Stone', and at second draft changed it to 'The Rocking Stone'. Once I had chosen the stone, already described above, as my key to the poem which, I knew, had been lying in wait for decades for its language, it was as if I had placed it in a sling and swung it hard – and I'm aware here of the biblical reference to another giant, another stone. 'The Rocking Stone' moved with its own momentum, or, to use its own history as a metaphor, once it had rocked too far it lost balance, and nothing could hold it back. For indeed, by the time the poem was written the logan stone had gone. After millennia of erosion it had fallen at last, in a storm I suppose, to be lost in the depths of the sea at the foot of the cliffs before I could write about it, although it was certainly there on the headland throughout my childhood and into my early twenties.

I took a sheet of paper and wrote: '*Llanthony. 2nd June 1990. On the headland is an absence, / where it fell, some winter night / between here and childhood. Since / I've searched the beach*'. Then I crossed out the four lines and tried again. The first sixteen words, as far as 'childhood', remained in every succeeding draft, though with different line-breaks, until the poem was published in May 1993. Not the stone but its absence became the poem's generating moment, Cordelia's 'nothing'. My own father had died before I was twenty. The stone had already left the sling. It was the 'airy nothing' to which I would try to give 'a local habitation and a name' (*A Midsummer Night's Dream*). I'd always wanted a brother, and a fantasy brother was the next best thing. Was the

giant brother Bendigeidfran /Goliath/father killed by the poem?
Can remembered life survive the fiction we make of it? Is this the
purpose and meaning of elegy? On the sixth sheet, dated 2 June,
is a version of 'The Stone' which concludes:

> balanced its mass so delicately,
> four thousand years withstanding weather
> like a dozing horse.[3]

The three lines remain in every draft until the poem reaches its
completion. The following four lines, which first appear in version
three, contain the exact words of the final published one:

> On the headland is an absence where it fell
> some winter night between here and childhood,
> and the sea's still fizzing
> over a bruise that will not heal.[4]

The poem then proceeds on an increasingly determined course,
through themes and phrases that will later develop into two whole
and separate poems, the first and third of the final sequence. In
draft four, almost all of both poems are there, tangled together, as
the ideas rush in too fast to sort them out. In a draft written later
that day, seven out of twelve of the lines that will conclude the
published sequence, 'The King of Britain's Daughter', are already
written:

> When I took you there,
> a pebble of basalt in my pocket,
> I showed you the white farm, the black beach,
> the empty headland where the stone
> balanced its mass so delicately,
> four thousand years withstanding weather
> like a dozing horse.[5]

---

3 'The King of Britain's Daughter'.
4 'The Stone', third version.
5 'The King of Britain's Daughter'.

For the sake of chronology I will return to the other half of the theme set at Hay – Motherland – and to the other poem I wrote on the first day. At the time I thought I would write eventually on both themes (in fact, I would, in a future book), and that if a long poem were completed, it would reflect both sides of the border, because at the time it seemed that the interesting area was the border itself, the scar, the edge of conflict and healing.

In pursuit of motherland I wrote 'Sunday'. The first image that came to me was that symbol of marriage and Sunday dinner, the wedding silver. From that came the golden question mark, the little hook that locked those old gilded leather cutlery cases, their lids lined with padded white satin under which bone-handled dinner and desert knives, two kinds of fork, silver soup and desert spoons were laid to rest all week in their beds of violet or cobalt velvet, sometimes 'Sylvo'-ed before being stored. Fish knives and forks, and tea spoons, were laid in separate boxes.

These are ceremonial objects, and Sunday was a special day. Many children in those days (the 1940s and 50s) found their parents' interpretation of these ceremonials differed. For my mother, Sunday lunch was the centrepiece. For my father, the day's pleasures lay in the freedom of the workshop, in mending and making things. For a child there was, in the air of such a day, such hope for familial magic that it must, ultimately, disappoint. To be with the two loved people offers the possibility of joy, maybe an outing, the healing of rifts. But Sunday is also where father, mother and child meet at the border where the fissures and the tensions are. It's where the barbed wire is. It ends in tears, of course.

'Sunday' was written on 3 June at Llanthony in two handwritten drafts and a typed one. The third draft is almost the same as the one which is published in the collection *The King of Britain's Daughter*. The house we lived in, from when I was about ten until I was an adult, had a basement. In the first draft I am in that basement, in my father's workshop, and my mother is 'upstairs', on the ground floor, 'unhooking the golden question mark'. In draft two the final version of the first two stanzas is decided, except that the earlier 'locked' has become 'unlocked', a moment of release instead of entrapment, maybe. The writing of the poem was an honest journey into remembering, an attempt at the accurate recapturing of detail, the spoons and forks 'powdery with *Sylvo*', the oiled bits of the drill, the colour of the oil. Then I recaught the day's emotions and found the miming cat among the more obvious remembered things, church bells, the smell of sprouts. Poetry is a hook for memory. Out of the excitement of writing emerged, to my surprise, 'the small horizon of the water-jug', the connecting looking-glass surfaces of water and mirror that must have remained from the sill and horizon of house and sea I had been preoccupied with in 'The Rocking Stone', and beyond which there was to be found another world. Water and mirror would lead me to the garden pond where I would find, resting at the edge, a stone. It seemed natural, an accurate memory though perhaps not from that particular day, that the child grieving over a spoilt Sunday would lie beside the water with the cat, 'inching a stone to the edge, until it fell'.

Since 'Sunday', the earliest version of 'The Rocking Stone', and the lines which would conclude 'The King of Britain's Daughter', all written and drafted in the few hours between reporting to an audience eager to know how we were getting on with the task, the writing had been interrupted by several public discussions. I recall describing to the audience the surprise I felt at the fall of the stone into the pond. I knew at the time that I was writing about pain and darkness, about a child sulking, but the final line came to me a split second before I could realise that I was foretelling the fall of the logan stone, the absence on the cliff, and the other absences and 'nothings' that the yet unwritten longer poem would contain. I recall taking a quick breath of excitement, a coming up for air, as image and understanding of the image filled me before the ink had dried on the page. At that moment the child in fantasy, and the real child I had been, (for it really did happen), became the storm that pushed a Neolithic boulder into the sea. It was in that moment of connection that the stone gained its full potency as a poet's object of desire, a weapon to slay a foe. The other symbol to set down its mark here is the horizon, which is to become so important not only in the sequence, but in the whole collection, *The King of Britain's Daughter*. The horizon will be as significant as the stone in the long sequential fatherland poem yet to be written. (Is it because I lived by the sea?)

In the salt-blind dining room
I levelled myself against the small horizon
of the water jug. The mirrors steadied.

Horizons are about the crossing of oceans, the track of light on the
sea, the path into the sunset taken by the Start-rite children in an
old advertisement, the two little figures in a Charlie Chaplin film
setting off on their adventures, the road through the magical peaks
in Rupert Bear books, storybook characters with their bundles on
sticks, off to seek their fortunes. I have elsewhere talked of how I
saw radio as my first travelling. At a turn of the tuning knob of the
radio (which stood on that other horizon, the windowsill) I could
hear the place-names and languages of faraway places. These glassy
levels, horizontals and verticals, are thrown by the wobble of tears
in the 'salt-blind' dining room.

In the outburst of a first idea, a few hours of work will bring a short
poem into being. To develop such an idea into something much
more, longer, deeper, more satisfying, something more is needed.
I have thought long about this in my efforts to help others with
their writing. The most potent source of energy for me is intense
concentration. It sounds so obvious that I wish I could find a more
striking word than 'concentration', without reaching for terms like
'meditation', which suggests something quasi-religious. However,
a creative concentration must be deep, uninterruptible, and self-
centred. The other useful intellectual tool is research. This could
mean reading, or looking, among other things. I would like to
broaden the idea of research here. For my purposes I needed factual
books, on geology for example, and maps of the coast. There are
often verbal treasures to be found in the language of geology, geog-
raphy, science and technology, a fresh vocabulary and a startling
imagery. But I need poetry too, and by broadening the meaning
of 'research' I include the necessity to nourish oneself with the
finest poetry in order to write it. Nothing is more inspiring than
the work of fine writers. In the early stages of all intense writing
periods I carry books around with me from room to room, and
many of these are poetry books. Beginners often express their fear
of imitating other writers, but reading which is sufficient in quan-
tity and richness is nourishing and thrilling. The true poet finds a

voice to join in the dialogue of poetry, and will strengthen in eloquence in the excitement of such discourse.

What excited the first words into life in 'The Stone' were the languages I'd heard in childhood, and the possibility of language that spoke from the stone itself. I began to consider the legend, and the metaphor it suggested, the levels of meaning it brought together, the significance it gave to the present. Images moved towards each other. Boulder / skim-stone / sun / sand-grain; horizon / sea, / windowsill; radio / father / voices / stories; war / giant / quarrels / storms. The possibility now occurred to me to connect the many-layered, much-sourced story with the living experience of the present. I felt there was a connection between the brother–sister relationship, of which I had no experience, and the father–daughter relationship which I knew. I would return to Fforest, now, in the present tense, addressing the listener, my partner, my companion, telling him the story. I hoped that this might make the poem immediate for myself and for the reader.

In any case there was no avoiding the poem now: the ideas were coming in too fast to record. I would attempt to parallel the legend of Branwen and Bendigeidfran with real life through remembering. I saw art but not artificiality in the idea, since the story of Branwen had been made my own. My father had given it to me. I noted themes for poems as they occurred. A few months after the Hay Festival I wrote in my notebook:

> shipwrecks and mysteries; *The Marie Celeste*; *The Titanic*: photograph of the shark in the ballroom, ships, 'Sparks' officer', [my father had been a merchant ships wireless officer for the Marconi company], Morse code, linking circles, limekilns, houseboat, Concorde, radios.

Research can always offer a fresh vocabulary, and a map of Pembrokeshire soon yielded rich geological language. I walked the cliffs and beaches again, rediscovering what I thought I had forgotten. I swam out into the bay and around the cliffs, searching for the drowned logan stone:

> Today I swim beyond the empty headland
> in search of the giant's stone.

Do I see it through green translucent water,
shadow of a wreck, a drowned man's shoulder, a clavicle
huge as a ship's keel wedged between rocks?[6]

Writing is itself a way to salvage memory. Staring at the page, beginning to set down the first marks, like drawing, and diving under the sea in search of the stone, set going submarine thoughts. Within this undersea which I have elsewhere called 'the other country' ('Seals', *Letting in the Rumour*), lies the archaeology of both the seabed and the subconscious. I soon remembered shipwrecks my father had told me about, or about which I had read. There were other forgotten, half-understood things down there, a memory of my mother, for instance, dressed up for a New Year's Eve dance, which brought with it an unaccountable sense of loss. The glittering ballgown merged with a beautiful and famous photographic image of a shark swimming down the staircase into the derelict ballroom of the *Titanic*:

a staircase in the sea
and something gleaming in the deepest water.[7]

I recalled the scientific knowledge my father had shared with me, especially on subjects like radio, sound, light, space, the stars. Sometimes he took me with him on his site-planning visits for the BBC to chapels, village halls, castles, marquees, even fields.

Outside in the graveyard
I collected frozen roses,
an alabaster dove with a broken wing
for my hoard in the long grass,

while he unreeled his wires down the aisle,
hitched the microphone to the pulpit
and measured silence with a quick chorus
from *The Messiah*.[8]

6 Poem 14, 'The King of Britain's Daughter'.
7 Poem 10, 'The King of Britain's Daughter'.
8 Poem IV of 'Radio Engineer', 'The King of Britain's Daughter'.

A remembered visit to a chapel with my father set going the poem
'Radio Engineer', itself a sequence of four poems, at the heart of
'The King of Britain's Daughter'.

> Staring into the starry sky, that time
> in the darkest dark of war and countryside,
> 'What is the stars?'
> my father asked,
>
> then told me that up there,
> somewhere between us and Orion,
> hangs the ionosphere, lower, closer at night,
> reflecting his long wave signals back to earth,
>
> light bending in water.
> But things get tight and close,
> words, music, languages
> all breathing together under that old *carthen*,
>
> Cardiff, Athlone, Paris
> all tongue-twisted up,
> all crackle and interference,
> your ears hearing shimmer
>
> like trying to stare at stars.[9]

The delightfully named Heaviside Layer, 'that old carthen' against
which longwave radio signals are bounced, (so named because it
was discovered by Professor Heaviside), and the old traditionally
woven Welsh wool *carthenni* weighing down the beds in my
grandmother's farm, had long ago merged and become metaphors
for each other in my mind.
  'Radio Engineer' ends thus:

> Still I can't look at stars,
> or lean with a telescope, dizzy, against the turning earth,

9 'The Heavidide Layer', from 'Radio Engineer', 'The King of Britain's
Daughter'.

without asking again, 'What is the stars?'
or calling 'Testing, testing' into the dark.

By the time the last stanza of 'Radio Engineer' arrives, I am alone.
I have no father. I am the older generation now. His voice testing
the microphone and the acoustics of a chapel is my voice shouting
into space 'Is anybody out there?' My father often quoted from
Sean O'Casey's *The Plough and the Stars*. Gazing up into the night
sky and saying, 'What is the stars?' was the nearest we, born into
a Welsh Baptist tradition but not practising it, got to questioning
the mysterious possibility of God. The significance of stars in the
dark sky, 'in the darkest dark of war and countryside', troubles
poem after poem in the sequence. In poem 9, 'Giants', Bendigei-
dfran is back, but this time he is stamping his raging foot not on
a rocky shore, but in space, bringing together legend and late-
twentieth-century technology, making myth out of breaking the
sound-barrier:

> Tonight, as Concorde folds her tern-wings back
> to take the Atlantic,
> I hear a giant foot stamp twice.
> You can still see the mark he made,
> a black space in the stars.

Bendigeidfran's footprint has become a negative, a space where
nothing is. When I first read aloud to myself the final lines of 'Radio
Engineer', I felt dizzy at what the words were telling me. I had
been aiming for a simple language, and to curb my natural extrav-
agance with words. I had hoped to cut a clean syntax out of stone
and horizon, to purge my work of adjectives and adverbs. For a
writer the language is everything and everything is in the language.
Ideas follow language. Symbolism collects about it. Metaphor
speaks through it. The horizon is the water-table of 'Anorexic' (a
poem in the collection *The King of Britain's Daughter*, but outside
the sequence). It is a windowsill, water-table, the surface of the
sea, the ionosphere, the lateral gossamer of a spider's web. In the
castle of Branwen's exile in Ireland, 'the rising sun / on the wall
like a crock of marigolds', refers, without first asking my permis-
sion, to a jar of marigolds on the farm windowsill of Fforest.

Finally, the stone has become the sun, the legendary apple, a pebble of amber, the game called 'skimstones', a rocking stone, all stones. It is the Neolithic stone lifted again to its place on the cliff at Fforest, the rising and the setting sun, the hot star by which we live. In the closing lines of poem 16 which concludes the sequence, language hands me a stone:

> Walking the beach
> we felt the black grains give
> and the sun stood
> one moment on the sea
> before it fell.

The Poetry of Stone: Pentre Ifan

Stones, hauled from the mountain, set upright, steadied and rammed tight into the ground to bear the great weight of the capstone. Seen from below across the fields against the sky, the cromlech is an awesome sight, yet familiar. We know it as we know the letters of the alphabet. It has become the very sign for the word 'stone'.

But it is not just a monument, not just an arrangement of huge stones. It is somehow, whatever we mean by the word, holy. A place sacred in the same way as the little Celtic church on the cliff above the sea at Mwnt, or the Cathedral at St Davids. It is the human mark on it and the human design of the stones that catch our breath. What vision impelled them beyond themselves, against the odds to go to such lengths of strength and ingenuity, to endure such hardship to bring vast blocks down from the mountain to build this tomb? In the fourth millennium BC, a group of Neolithic people were moved to collaborate on the mighty work of raising one of our earliest public monuments. They had settled the slope at the eastern end of the Preseli mountains to cultivate crops and keep their animals. Yet food and shelter were not enough. Above them, the stones of Carn Meini, an outcrop on the hill, stood ready for quarrying. It is fine granite, hard igneous rock. Ancient upheavals hurled molten stone from deep in the mantle of the earth. All sedimentary rock, formed later, has eroded away, leaving this, the hardest stuff, jutting in giant slabs against the skyline.

Beside me on the table are three fragments of planet earth: a granite sett – igneous white stone speckled black and winking with quartz; a small block of purple slate from Penrhyn – five-hundred-million year-old metamorphic rock marked by nothing but the slate-man's tools and the ice that split it as neatly as a book falling open at the page you were reading; and a tablet of limestone about three hundred million years old – a photograph of a moment in the life of the warm shallows of the littoral before the seas withdrew and left it high and dry somewhere in what is now Derbyshire. The limestone is cut and polished, teeming with sea lilies, a stilled seethe of primitive life-forms and shell fragments, and what looks like one very small trilobite as real and wide awake as if it lived. It is like footage of old Movietone.

If I set two of the stones on end and place the other on top, they make a cromlech. Close to my desk, leaning against bookshelves, is a life-size limestone hare, sculpted by Meic Watts, its polished body another moment frozen from the life of an ancient sea, 'a premonition of stone' from the Palaeozoic:

> In its limbs lies the story of the earth,
> the living ocean, then the slow birth
> of limestone from the long trajectories
> of starfish, feather-stars, crinoids and crushed shells
> that fill with calcite, harden, wait for the quarryman,
> the timed explosion and the sculptor's hand.[1]

I've returned again and again to the poetry of stone. In 'The Sundial', one of my first published poems, I see not only stone but megalith as I watch my young son 'calculating/ the mathematics of sunshine'. But it was poetry itself that surprised more from the domestic incident than I had expected. From watching a child make a sundial out of a circle of paper, marking the hours with twelve pebbles, language, and poetry's stranger impulse, found the parallel: that the child, like the primitive man in the Neolithic, is finding his way in a world with no maps, that the mud-pie, the sandcastle, the pebble and driftwood house, are how a child learns all over again what early man discovered, that these materials are for human use, art, and imagination. Out of the stuff of the earth we can make pots and axe-heads, dens, cathedrals, a sundial to

---

1 Gillian Clarke, 'The Stone Hare', *Making the Beds for the Dead* (Carcanet, 2004).

calculate the hours of the day and seasons of the year, a telescope to observe the stars. Years ago in Samarkand I was shown the forerunner of the telescope, part of a ruined fifteenth-century observatory. The sextant was a tunnel of stone, like a huge open chimney, but slanting from earth to sky, revealing, square by square, the map of the stars as the Earth turned in space. In the Boyne Valley in Ireland the famous passage grave of Newgrange shows that its Stone Age builders needed to know exactly when the shortest day occurred, to calculate and mark it precisely. They used a beam of sunlight. At dawn at the winter solstice the rising sun sends a ray of light through a slit in the portal to touch the wall of the chamber. On no other day of the year can that happen. Newgrange, Stonehenge and the observatory in Uzbekistan are milestones on the road to human understanding of mathematics.

The granite sett, the oldest of my three samples, the enduring material that has made some of our most impressive megaliths, comes from Pembrokeshire. It was cut to pave a city courtyard or street, 'a floor hewn from the batholith'. Monuments made from limestone have been badly worn away by time and weather. They loll in their circles like melting snowmen. The granite ones seem untouched by time or weather. No wonder the rock was prized.

My three rocks tell Earth's story. They mark time from nothing to inert stone and on to early life, and all that the word 'life' promised, and threatened. Abraham, Jesus, Mohammed. Dante, Mozart. Hitler. My children. Their children, one of whom is named Ifan. The spotted woodpecker at the bird feeder, now, and the now-ness of that flight of lapwings over the fields. Their small cries.

Igneous, metamorphic, sedimentary rock. How I loved my *Guide to Minerals, Rocks and Fossils*. I loved its language, the names of rock. Earth took its time with rock. It took ages. Then life began, fidgeting and wriggling for an unimaginably long, slow time, for ages, aeons, chrons. It is natural to be drawn to stone. It is human to stoop and pick up a pebble glowing among all the others on the beach, then another more beautiful than the first. Soon pockets are full and one must choose the best example of the red, the rust-gold, the green. There's a pure white one, a smooth grey with speckles or a ridged band of quartz, a veined blue. They can't all be carried away. At home in my room as a child I spent hours sorting stones into spirals and rows according to colour and size, counting, grading, arranging them on every available surface. Ga in the farm never minded my pebbles. Back in South Wales my mother was more houseproud. '*You* don't have to dust!' she complained. '*You* don't have to dust!' I'd reply.

Dust. Ashes to ashes, dust to dust. Water washes stone away. It didn't wash me away. There was no sign that my skin was any the less for the hours I spent in the sea. That was the mystery. Rock, even granite, turns to dust in the wind and the rivers. Stones are sucked and licked and turned by the sea until they are shingle, then sand, grit, sediment. The sediment settles, lies flat or slumps into the sea and turns again to stone. Waves have spent all of time making pebbles, their salt tongues hollowing caves, undermining cliffs. Could I suck a pebble until it dissolved like a sweet? Would there be, at the very last moment, a seed, as in an aniseed ball? What would you grow from the seed in a stone? I knew, as a child, that crystals grew, that they accrued, multiplied and made themselves in the dark. The seed of a stone is a grain of sand, millions laid down, hardening again to make sedimentary rock which will, in turn, in the lick of wind and water wear away, ground into sand again. And so on and on reshaping the world, its bumps and hollows, its soils, allowing each plant to evolve in a particular locality, thriving on nutrients and conditions apt to its needs. You can taste rock, in spring water, in wine, in a beetroot pulled from the earth and simmered till its skin just peels away. You taste it in all salad leaves pulled from the earth and eaten at once. You taste it in steamed spinach.

The igneous tuffs and granites of the Preseli hills, the oldest rocks in Dyfed, their craggy shapes against the sky above sloping fields, are characteristic of the landscape of Pembrokeshire. Carn Meini, thrown from the Earth's mantle as it was forming thousands of millions of years ago, and Pentre Ifan, between them mark moments in the making of the planet, and the story of early humankind. I knew Carn Meini, from which Pentre Ifan's granite came, was the source of the inner circle of 'bluestones' at Stonehenge. But what were 'bluestones'? And why did the builders of Stonehenge think them so special that, according to a likely theory, they bore them by sea around the coast to the Bristol Channel, up the Severn estuary to the Avon, and up-river to Salisbury Plain? Yet the term 'bluestone' is not used in my old *Guide to Minerals, Rocks and Fossils*. Archaeologists and geologists don't talk the same language, and neither explain the term. However, Carn Meini granite, a mixture of rhyolite and a spotted dolerite with a slightly blue colour – at last, somewhere, I found it described as 'blue' – made the excellent polished stone axes which we know Neolithic people used. Axes made from Carn Meini stone have been found at megalithic sites in Ireland. To the seafarers of the Stone Age crossing to and from Ireland, Carn Meini must have been the first and the last sight of Wales. It was both landmark and lure, as it was to me as a child in my father's car driving to the coast, looking out for the first glimpse of the sea.

I passed no childhood day without the company of stones, without a pebble in my pocket, without using the sea-smoothed boulders of a beach as stepping stones to the sea, or playing in sand, or trudging through shingle, picnicking at a megalith, or leaning against the sun-warmed rocking stone on the cliff at Fforest to read, or draw, or write my diary. When I put my ear to it I could hear the stone purr like the sea in a shell; I could feel the Neolithic in the stone, like touching the arches when a train crosses a viaduct.

The port of Barry close to where we lived in South Wales was bombed by the Germans during the Second World War. Once I was old enough – say, four years old – my father took me to Fforest to stay with Ga. Often one or more of my father's three sisters were there too. My mother, pregnant with my sister, and then with a newborn baby to care for, chose to risk the bombs to stay home in Barry with electricity, a proper bathroom and a hospital close by. Later they all came for a few weeks in summer, but I would not be persuaded to go home with them. When the war ended, and I started school, we went to Fforest for all our holidays.

Here myth intervenes. First a personal one. It must be a memory made of layers of experience, story, snapshot, hearsay and imagination, images laid down one on the other like sedimentary rock. I see a picnic with my father at Pentre Ifan, myself playing close to the cromlech, the blue sea through its huge windows. It was like a little church, its stone roof balanced like a feather on its pillars, each window literally the wind's eye. The oldest roof in Wales, the oldest building, yet not so holy you had to whisper, not too holy for cheese sandwiches and *bara brith* spread with Ga's salty home-churned butter, a bag of windfall apples and a flask of sweet tea.

The sea as seen from Pentre Ifan is a distant blue line, a ribbon of Cardigan Bay beyond the sands of Newport and the black shingle of Fforest and numerous other little coves and bays a few miles away. It is difficult to date that first visit to Pentre Ifan. Why do I not remember the temporary structure of oak beams raised to hold it steady during the archaeological excavations conducted by W.F. Grimes and his team? Have I erased the wounded stones, and replaced it with the cromlech as I later encountered it? Or have I confused a picnic at the cromlech with a picnic at another megalith, the rocking-stone at Fforest? Grimes had the oak structure erected in 1937 to support the monument ready for excavation of the ground close to the portal. The work was interrupted by the outbreak of war in 1939, and the strengthening beams were left in place for over a decade. I was a new-born, an infant, a small child, a schoolgirl during that time. Ga died in 1945 and after her death it was into the care and company of my aunts and uncle that my father delivered me every school holiday. To make a memory of that picnic at the cromlech, maybe I have remembered Pentre Ifan unbandaged from its war wounds some time in the 1950s to stand whole against the sky and sea. To accompany it, I must have summoned my grandmother from an earlier time, shaking a feather mattress at an open window, pegging white sheets on a line. That picnic scene contains elements that cannot have existed together. The rocking stone, or logan stone, balanced on the south cliff at Fforest is the more likely site, just a walk away from the house down to the shore and along the beach, across the river, along a muddy path through woods, and out on the open track that went firm and dry up the cliff between bracken to the headland, the perfect place for a picnic. There we'd sit on dry, sheep-cropped grass, lean against the warm stone, eat our bread and cheese and watch the sea. We looked for the head of a seal, or a ship on the horizon. Here a public myth sails in from Ireland. We take possession of it. It is my father's gift to me, stolen from the Mabinogion and its traditional associations. Now it is ours. A ship might be one of Bendigeidfran's, returning from Ireland after the tragic, ill-fated mission to rescue Branwen. According to my father Bendigeidfran would one day come to claim his pebble. With any luck I'd be there when it happened. In imagination, in family mythology, and perhaps in megalithic history, Pentre Ifan and the rocking stone at Fforest are connected.

Years later, when I returned to the cliff at Fforest, there was no stone. Just 'an absence' on the headland.

I swam out into the bay to the headland and dived. The waters of Pembrokeshire are clear as glass. Did I find the giant's stone? Nothing.

Is this how we make myth, and make sense of the world? Pentre Ifan was a place of wonder to me. I remember, from more visits than I can count between childhood and now, the mystery of how the megalith is grounded, a great weight on the earth, yet how the vast capstone seems scarcely to touch the uprights. You can see light pass almost all the way between orthostats and capstone. You'd swear a piece of paper could slide between them. It makes light of gravity. It is a place where the stone from the earth has been hacked from the mountain, handled and hauled and hoisted by human hands, showing how already, in the Stone Age, we were architects, inventing, working together to make what archaeologists have called a public building. The orthostats have been chosen with care. The two portal stones match and curve to echo each other. This is no crude, basic building. It is design. Long ago, men chose these stones, brought them from the mountain, lifted them into place, stood back, saw what we see now, and were satisfied. In 1624, in a piece entitled 'Elements of Architecture', Sir Henry Wotton wrote:

> In architecture as in all the operative arts, the end must direct the operation. The end is to build well. Well building hath three conditions. Commodity, firmness and delight.

Pentre Ifan is commodious enough to contain mountain and sky, the distant sea, six thousand years of stories and all the mythology a father could pass to a child. It is the very epitome of firmness, originating as it does from the Earth itself, and holding for so long its rootedness upon it. And delight? It is the one, perfect design for a cromlech. High enough for a horse and rider to pass beneath it, as an early illustration shows, other cromlechs are squat as toad-stools in comparison. Pictogram. Portal. The most elegant initial letter in a book of stone.

Voice of the Tribe

One of the most moving poems I know by heart is the one in which the American poet Richard Wilbur addresses six lines to the poets of ancient Etruria, a people and a language wiped out, lock, stock and barrel, by the Romans. He urges his brother Etruscan poets, long dead, to 'dream fluently', and tells how they took in their language with their mothers' milk, little knowing that their poetry was doomed as soon as written. If a language dies, its poetry dies. 'Joining world with mind', they wrote their verse:

> Like a fresh track across a field of snow,
> Not reckoning that all could melt and go.[1]

A lost language represents the obliteration of a culture, a monument rubbed clean of words. There are no words for it. It is too sad for words. We are speechless, struck dumb. English abounds with idiom to describe the ache of wordlessness, though its native speakers are, on the whole, too confirmed in monolingualism fully to understand what those English words are saying, To speak two languages is to be in two minds, to see both sides. 'Welsh' means them, the strangers; its translation, 'Cymry' means us, we who belong. It must make a difference to a poet to live in a bilingual country, to hear two drums beating.

My first favourite word, they tell me, was 'pandemonium'. I was two years old and understood only that I must stop making it upstairs. I searched the blue room for the thing with the beautiful name. Nothing but a new bed, with a blue and white counter-

---

1 Richard Wilbur, 'To the Etruscan Poets', *New and Collected Poems* (Faber, 1989).

pane, and a lake flashing between the curtains its gleaming,
ominous smile, like an old aunt by whom I might be swallowed.
   The sound of foghorns. The blackout siren. Waves breaking.
The deep silence of the lake. I grew up in a Tower of Babel.
English was the proper tongue. The world spoke it, according to
my mother. She spoke it to me, so it was my mother tongue. Yet
the family language was Welsh. It was, literally, the familiar
language. Nain and Taid, my North Wales grandparents, spoke it,
Mamgu, my South Wales grandmother spoke it, and my dead
Tadcu spoke it to God. My father tongue was Welsh, the only
language ever used between my father and his mother; for all four
grandparents and all my ancestors as far back, I suppose as the sixth
century, when, as far as we know, something like Welsh as we
know it began, it was the language of speech, thought and dream.
In this universe of Welsh my young, beautiful, aspirational mother
held her head high and chose the aristocrat's language, the tongue
she had spoken at the grammar school, tongue of the landowner,
the landlord, the official, the bureaucrat, Winston Churchill, the
King, and the BBC London Home Service. She looked down on
the Welsh Home Service from which our family income came.
'Radio Cymru!' she scoffed, (the 'a' short, as in 'hat'), 'Radio is an
English word'. I knew better. It was Latin, my father told me, and
therefore international, the world's word. I knew better too than
to argue. I kept my head down, sensing at the earliest age that this
was an area of tension, a minefield of pride and loss that language
had become in our tribe. Welsh became for her the forbidden
tongue, and I knew then that I would disobey her, and would, one
day, look into the dark room and find it, that I would discover its
gossip, its forbidden literature, the secrets my aunts and cousins
told each other about our history. It had a whiff of danger about
it, and still I hear it as if, as well as being a tongue to speak and
understand, it were a secret, tribal tongue, spoken by grown-ups
while I listen, my ear to the wall. I still dream of falling asleep
before the iron range in one of the family farms, a pet lamb in a
box by the fire, hearing Welsh, and the clatter of buckets on a flag-
stone floor.
   Outside, in the seaport where we lived then during the war, we
heard American, an incomprehensible gibberish. The American
servicemen couldn't speak our language either, so they changed it

to suit themselves. Some of the US servicemen were based at Rhydlafar – the ford over talking waters, or the ford of talk – but they couldn't say it so they called it Red Lava, which became its common name to this day, its old mystery lost, the secret whispered at the ford forgotten.

I was to learn, much later, that the imperialist process begins with language. You are powerful. You are superior. You have more money, more and bigger guns. So you assume that you speak a superior language, and that it is superior because your culture, your literature, your civilisation, your system of government are superior. My mother never understood this. To the end of her life she, brought up in a hard-up, Welsh-speaking, tenant-farming family, would say if she heard me on the radio, 'You were good. You didn't sound too Welsh.' Too Welsh would be even worse than being Welsh in the first place. In *Translations*, his play about the British Army's making of the Ordnance Survey maps of Ireland in the nineteenth century, Brian Friel, the Irish playwright, shows how a peasant people who spoke Gaelic, and could read Latin and Greek, were thought to be ignorant savages by the British officers, because they could not speak English.

Apart from the time with Ga in my first two years when we all lived together, I was given only English in my childhood, English nursery rhymes, BBC Children's Hour, A.A. Milne, Beatrix Potter, Enid Blyton, a literature where, occasionally, among the blond English middle class heroes and corn-haired heroines, a Welsh peasant child, black-haired and speaking pidgin English, would appear like a changeling in a country house adventure, or as a servant boy no one trusted, or a Gypsy boy who muttered spells. In films they were always policemen.

I wrote my address in my first school books: Flatholm, Cold Knap, Barry, Glamorgan, Wales, Great Britain, Europe, Earth, the Universe. Flatholm took its Old Norse name from an island in the Bristol Channel – not the Cardiff Channel, even as La Manche is translated not as the Sleeve, but as the English Channel. Thus I knew England as the bigger, more important place. Flatholm, and its sister island, Steepholm, could be seen from our house, which felt a bit like another island, the lake water so close, and the sea talking all night from two directions: mumbling on the Pebbly Beach, shushing in the Little Harbour, and between these two voices the lake's deep, dark, reflecting silence, like the silence of old, blotched mirrors that remember everything.

To the island house in the peninsular town, along airwaves, and my father's intricate webs of wire, came Europe, its languages unravelling into the back of a wireless set. Its tongues, sounds and beautiful names dwelt in the dim, green light of the set, their syllables, Paris, Luxembourg, Hilversum, just as real as the England I could see across the water on a clear day, and London no farther and no closer than Berlin. Wherever we were, at home in South Wales, with Ga on the farm, or at Nain's in the North, there was a wireless in every room, and Medusan coils of wire pushed behind every sideboard. Overhead swept the weather – the glory of living in the Atlantic airstream is weather's variousness – and every manifestation of nature had a weather forecast to its name in Welsh and English. In English it rains cats and dogs. In Welsh it rains knives and forks. In English the night is dark as a cellar. In Welsh it's dark as a cow's stomach. In English literature 'rock' is symbolically male and 'water' female, but in Welsh, 'rock' is a feminine noun, 'water' masculine. The space between the languages is as dynamic as the huge currents of the Severn estuary between the two shores.

The landscape where I grew up, its name, history and mythology, were Welsh. Under Cardigan Bay lies the drowned land of Cantre'r Gwaelod. The stream where Lleu, Blodeuwedd's husband, turned into an eagle and perched in an oak for a year and a day, is still known as Nant Lleu. An English friend was stunned to read the message 'Rhiannon was 'ere, July 1989', carved by a local girl into a mountain stone near Harlech. He thought it the ghostly manifestation of a mythological heroine. The Mabinogion, the ancient legends of Britain, find their shrunken topography in Wales, stories which are largely forgotten and neglected in England.

Two sea-sounds, two languages, two versions of the world, of myself, of history, of what should be valued, of what culture and civilisation are: English, the mother always sure she's right and knows what's best; Welsh, the father, luring to adventures beyond certainty, inclining me to the greater world. When we are most true to ourselves we are most universal, as Chekhov proves. To the ear of the Welsh writer in English comes the beat of two drums, whether or not the writer is fluently bilingual. The Welsh language, like the landscape, is always on the skyline or at the end of the street in a name. Few parts of Wales are entirely without Welsh, or hills.

These linguistic riches, tensions and confusions lead me occasionally to use a Welsh word in a poem written in English. A case in point is '*dŵr*' in 'The Water-Diviner'. I hope that this does not annoy monolingual English readers. I regard it as sharing the old British tongue. *Dŵr*, water, is a common British word, and it used to ride the sides of the old Welsh Water Board vans for anyone to read. On one side, 'Dŵr Cymru', on the other, 'Welsh Water', and on both the logo of blue and green waves. Even the logo is significant to a Welsh speaker, because the word '*glas*' means both blue and green. This makes complete sense in a western British landscape, where water and hills are indeed, both blue and green, and those two words are scarcely more useful than one to describe the range of colours from ink through purples, lavenders, greys, and all the greens in the world, to describe mountains. *Dŵr* is a word evolved from *dŵfr*, the 'f' (pronounced, as in 'of', as the English 'v') retained in the plural *dyfroedd*, waters. It lives on still in southern England in the town of Dover, reminding us that the British language was Welsh. '*Dŵr*' was the right word for 'The Water-Diviner', the word on my tongue, the word that, when I blew into the hose dipped into the 54-foot deep borehole down to the water source, the earth called back. I blew. The earth shouted '*dŵr*', elongated to an echoing call from the deep earth. The water diviner used a metal rod. I later learned to divine, to guess water, since that day in the great drought of 1976, when water was found in our garden. After hours unsuccessfully pacing up and down with a forked hazel twig, suddenly a shock ran into my arms, then it grew stronger until the twig snapped and my palms were scratched. 'The Water-Diviner' is about finding language, finding poetry. You can't always do it, but once it has come you are caught. No wonder men have talked of the Muse, seductive, sensual. The pen over paper can sometimes have the power of a hazel twig over hidden water.

In the second poem in the water series, 'Syphoning the Spring', 'the water comes / like birth-water', and if readers find something sexual there I hope they find both body and gender, the feminine noun 'rock' opening, the masculine 'water' rising, the Muse androgynous, poetry coming.

> So that it dares to fall clear, for it wants
> to fall, to give itself, knowing the risk.

I realise, as I write, how often I have used falling water, or simply falling, to praise the giving of the self. In 'Falling', for instance, a poem that only declared itself to be a love poem once it was written,

> Falling's a trust game. Fall simply
> like a baby, nothing breaks.

Not meaning alone, but rhythm and stress and what we call accent make a language fit for poetry, and render it untranslatable. Welsh stresses the penultimate syllable, but in the ultimate syllable, when spoken aloud, I hear the voice take a semi-tonal step up the scale. The stress is strong, but the slight rise in note in the second syllable is so slight as to be almost indiscernible, as in *Ow*ain, *Dy*lan, and the single penultimate stress in place-names like Dolg*ell*au, Mach*yn*lleth, Llany*stum*dwy, Llanr*hai*adr-ym-*moch*nant. They are difficult, to be sure, as they use consonantal sounds unknown in English. Yet the rise and fall of the note, and the placing of the stress, are the characteristics of my second language which contribute to what is called the lilt in the Welsh voice speaking English. The famous voices of Dylan Thomas and Richard Burton illustrate the stress and tune of Welsh, colouring the tones of spoken English. They would have pronounced not 'diffcty' (difficulty), as in much BBC English, but *difficulty*; not 'secetry' (secretary) but *secretary*. All syllables and consonants are weighted with importance in much Welsh-English, adding to the pleasurable savouring of each part of a word. Once in a while, working with children in a poetry class, I see a child shiver, or smile with pleasure. I see the mouth move, tasting a phrase. I see how they like their own words. There, perhaps, is the poet tonguing the language, like a flautist, a wine-taster. Language 'joining world with mind'.

So how could a poet who hears two drums beating be confined to listening only to one? Why deny the double joy of reading Shakespeare and Dafydd ap Gwilym, or using the known word just because it belongs to a minority language, the oldest living European tongue, containing literary riches quite out of proportion to its number of speakers? Welsh is a modern language, spoken today by under a million people. It's the only Celtic tongue spoken across all classes, ages and education, sometimes the dominant language in whole towns and communities. At the time of writing, of all the Celtic tongues it has the best chance of surviving, an unbroken chain since the Dark Ages, before the Romans subdued the island of Britain and enriched the British language with the *caer* (fort), the *pont* (bridge), the *ffos* (ditch) and the *ffenestr* (window).

Out of all this pleasure and the need to feel again and again the electric connection between the deepest waters and the hovering hand with its hazel twig or pen, come a poet's responsibilities to mediate the world between those who'll be reading the poems and those whose world is being voiced. A poet is the voice of the tribe. A long Welsh tradition, at least fourteen centuries old and with a literature to prove it, has taught us that a voice and a few scribes are needed. Their job was to record, to recite genealogies, to write a people's history, to conjure sun and rain gods, to bring spring, to endure winter, to remember, to name, to list, to mythologise experience, to praise God, princes, victories, love and nature, to seduce, lament, persuade, elegise, console and celebrate. The two literatures of Wales have been the people's journal. This is not quite the same role as the one English literature has played, where apart from the ballads, poetry has had a grander purpose. To generalise, people without much advanced, formal education in Wales are more likely to be aware of poetry and of poets than their social equals in England. All this makes a poet ordinary in Wales, someone who crafts poetry. As such a Welsh poet is as likely to be asked to write a verse for a birthday or a gravestone as receive a commission from the BBC for a radio ode, or a poem to use on television for the Rugby World Cup. Even the Poets Laureate of England have not much used their role to keep the people's journal, to lament the loss of millions of trees in the hurricanes that swept Britain in the 1980s, the deaths in disasters, the sinking of a ferry boat, the crushing of a football crowd, the loss of jobs, the poisoning of lakes and rivers.

Anthony Conran does the job superbly in his fine poem, 'Elegy for the Welsh Dead in the Falklands War', where he uses the form of the sixth-century *Gododdin* by the poet Aneurin, listing a particular group of Welshmen who died in the shelling of one ship, to lament the folly and tragedy of war and of young lives lost for nothing. It is a fierce, politically committed poem, as was its early-sixth-century predecessor.

From where I write I see a landscape open like a book, a landscape of valleys and hills. I can see a hamlet a mile away, and when night falls I will see its lit windows, and the lights of cars coming and going from the farms. I know the names of the farms and cottages, and those who live in them. I can name the fields on my side of the valley, and a few on the other side. Valleys, and a land that is tilted to face its neighbour, make for familiarity and open lives, rather like neighbourliness of face to face terraced streets. It encourages an already talkative people, a people curious to know each other's business, to question the stranger. If you want a quiet journey on a train travelling into Wales, they say, don't catch the eye of your fellow passengers. I have heard of the secretiveness of people from the Fens, the passivity of the residents of flat Suffolk, the silence of the Finns, the blarney of the Irish. These are stereotypes, but there's something in it. Landscape and history shape us. Wales is less in thrall to a class system than England. My late coalminer father-in-law loved poetry, classical music and opera. The South Wales miner, before the pits were closed by the Thatcher government of the 1980s, was famously literate and cultured, with a passionate desire to see his children educated. Those were the days of the chapels, the great male voice choirs, the drama groups, the debating societies, the miners' libraries. Somewhere among these generalisations lie truths that cast light on the position of the poet as a voice still heard in Wales.

But poetry is personal and individual too, and it shimmers with private secrets. A favourite word is 'perihelion' – the closest point to the sun in the journey of a planet or a comet. I drop it into the well and listen, looking, at the same time, at the mind's surface. I tell myself a fairy story in which Echo and Reflection fall in love, but Echo is blind, and Reflection a mute. When the story is told, it might teach me something of the word's search for its sister, the idea's quest for a voice. I am two years old, listening to the sea and searching for uproar and confusion in the abode of demons, in a blue and white room at the rim of a bottomless lake; and I'm an adult searching the sky for comets and trying to pick out from the background hiss on my radio the sound of the last echoes of the big bang that created the universe, still reverberating in space.

> In the sling of its speed the comet
> flowers to perihelion over the chimney.

> I hold the sky to my ear to hear
> pandemonium whispering.

A Journal

A White Page

January

On the first day of January I open a new journal and mark the clean page with a date, location, a first sentence. New Year's Day 2007. It is always an unlined, hardback black book, three inches by five, with acid-free paper. The first words print the field of snow. I relish the moment, the pen, the white page.

It is cold. There is a white frost on the grass. The sky is so pale a blue it might be white. A high passenger jet heading west for the Atlantic leaves its trail drifting on the sky like a kite string someone let go. A hare lopes across the horizon of Allt Maen's field, pauses and is gone. Long ago, when we slept up the ladder in the croglofft, we woke once on a spring morning to see, framed by the coincidence of the tiny gable window, a pair of hares dancing in the field. Another chance sighting, another time, saddened by news of the death of a neighbour's son, we walked up the lane and leaned on a gate to look over the fields. David lifted the binoculars and focused on our little larch wood, half a mile away. He gasped and passed them to me. There, brought close, a pair of fox cubs playing. The balance of things.

The hare leaves its shape on my retina and in my mind like the jet trail. Siani, the border collie, ignores hares because they are not sheep. On four occasions Meg, my late springer spaniel, brought home a young hare, once a tiny leveret, all unharmed in her soft, wet mouth.

The weather-people keep talking of a once-in-twenty-years hard winter, like 1947, '62, '83, coming any year now. Such talk makes my heart beat faster. The drama of extreme weather is both fearful and thrilling. These past few years it has come to nothing

more than a few weeks of dry, icy weather. Usually frost is kept at
bay in the west by the temperate air of the Atlantic, but when
winter anti-cyclones stall over the North Sea, the Atlantic holds
its breath. Snow falls to the east, while we lie under iron frost,
snowfall held back by the hills.

Twice it snows enough to make travelling difficult. Once David
is caught in a snowstorm and has to leave the car and walk miles
home. The other time we are on the westward journey home from
Cardiff, the day after seeing *The Marriage of Figaro* at the Wales
Millennium Centre. We stay overnight, and wake to a rare fall of
snow over the city, Queen Street purified, white civic buildings
unclean above their snowy lawns. After lunch and a city prowl we
deliver our old car and collect our new (to us) car from the garage.
Homebound in falling snow, all is well along the M4, the dual
carriageway, the country roads, until we reach the last mile. The
new car crawls, slewing slightly on the last steep hill with its ghostly
name, Rhiw Amwisg – hill of the shroud, or cloak. It's a bad place
to get stuck as the road is narrow and twisting. We only make it
because of a cunning device on the Swedish car which we had not
expected we would need so soon. The car 'knows' when it must
adjust to the depth of snow, or to any snow at all. The device kicks
in and the car carries us safely up the hill and home on the final
stretch.

New Year's Day 1970, when this house was still in a ruinous state
and fit only for summer camping, our late farmer-neighbour,
Hywel, telephoned us in Cardiff. In Ceredigion there had been a
fall of snow in the night, and a violent thunderstorm. A pony had
been killed in a field. A huge thunderclap broke over the farm roof
and a fireball blazed down the chimney into Hywel's bedroom
leaving flames and a scorched trail across the wallpaper. Next
morning Hywel was out in his pick-up to check his sheep. The
lane between his farm and our house was white with unmarked
snow, until he reached our gate. There, in the middle of the road,
with not a mark leading to it, were signs of disturbance as if, he

said, 'a pig had been rooting in the snow on the road'. Then the 'beast' had ploughed under the gate, across the drive and up the bank, burning a gouge out of the trunk of our sycamore tree. Later, we hoped to find a meteorite in the grass. We found nothing but a three-foot-by-two black scar healing on the trunk of the tree.

I think of Marged, after the death of her grandfather, Benni, and then her aunt, Nani, alone in this house in the winter of 1930. Rising in the dark to milk her cow, to draw water from the spring, to light her fire, what dark days and long, cold nights she must have endured. The darkness. The silence. The loneliness. Poor Marged! No wonder one winter, when she had flu, she hanged herself in despair, here, in this house, for the want of a welfare state.

We and the children had a glimpse into the life of the rural poor of the 1930s and earlier, when we camped here soon after we bought the smallholding from Hywel. We paid £450 for it, an old longhouse in a ruinous state, condemned, uninhabited for decades and therefore, though we did not know it then, ineligible under local authority planning rules for permission to be restored and lived in. Unaware of rules, we mended the roof, had the old rotten sash windows copied and replaced, got the chimney rebuilt and the walls made safe. We spent our holidays walking the land, fetching water from the spring and collecting wood by day, and reading by oil-lamp light and a big open fire in the evenings. It was fun. The children were excited by the walks in the woods, the log fires, the ghosts. I remember hearing my young daughter say to her brothers, 'Let's pretend she's our mother and we are the woodcutter's children.' They lived through books, as I did as a child, playing out their imagined stories in a place where poverty was not difficult to imagine.

I wanted to try, for the first time in my life, to live alone. I wanted a glimpse of insight into what it had been like for Marged, how she and her kind had lived without electricity, indoor running water, a bathroom, and all that we take for granted as our right. In 1984 I accepted the post as Poet in Residence at the University of

Lampeter. Despite the primitive state of the house I decided to move in. I wanted the experience of living alone in winter in Marged's house. It was almost a romantic idea, and it excited me. David was working as an architect in Aberystwyth, a 45-minute drive away. He and I had been commuting between Cardiff and Ceredigion each weekend while I was teaching at Newport College of Art. The children were at university, art college, or gigging round the country with a band in a van. I was ready for an adventure. Solitude in a primitive house in winter, but not too far from David and, if necessary, rescue and a visit at the weekend, would be a fresh white page.

It was the winter of the miners' strike and cold when we moved in, Meg, my springer spaniel, and I. The first snow fell in November. To keep the stove permanently burning I bought German coal, and felt guilty about it, but the heat of the stove warmed the room and rose into the croglofft above, where I slept without anxiety as long as Meg was quiet, sleeping in her bed at the foot of the ladder. Tractors on the move kept the lanes clear, so I was never cut off. The house was still primitive – there was no electricity, no bathroom, no indoor toilet – but we'd made it sound and weatherproof, and it was surprisingly simple to get a phone connected (one of the many compromises I made to the solo living plan). I had a calor gas cooker, a wood- or coal-burning stove, candles and oil lamps. It was a dark house even during daylight hours, so I had a large roof-window installed in the croglofft room up the ladder, where I would sleep, and write at a table under the window. The small sash window in the living room faced east and let in little light. The days were short. I powered a primitive computer with a car battery charged by a small wind turbine, and learned the hard way that when the wind stops blowing, there is no power.

Eight years earlier, when the spring had dried up in the drought of 1976, we had consulted a water diviner. Diviner is a good word for the magic of dousing. He 'divined' a powerful source fifty-four feet under the garden; we had a bore-hole drilled, and water rose with a deep bass sound like a syllable spoken by a bullfrog. Something like its own name in Welsh, 'dŵr'. Soon it was piped into a tap in the house, cold and clean. What a marvellous thing it seemed! It had to be heated in pans and kettles kept always filled

on the flat top of the iron stove, but at least sweet water rose out
of the deep earth below the garden into my tap.

Did I learn how Marged lived? No, but I thought of her a lot,
and constantly imagined her life as I measured it against my own.
I learned about silence, independence, solving my own problems,
not being afraid of the dark, of sleeping alone miles from a neigh-
bour with only a dog for company.

That winter I set off each morning in my Renault 4 (another
compromise!) between snowy hedge banks for the half-hour drive
to Lampeter. The university gave me a room on the ground floor
of a terraced house opposite the main college building. The Chap-
lain had a flat in the house, and – another cop-out, this! – I
gratefully accepted his offer of the daily use of his shower. It was
a warm, bright room facing the college grounds and the hills
beyond. People brought me their poems and stories, students,
people from the town and outlying countryside, and every
Tuesday night a group gathered to share work, discussion and
ideas. So began the Lampeter Writers' Workshop, still going strong
today. Recently one of the founding members of the group said,
'Remember The Writing Room?' We used it for years, my posses-
sion of the keys to that room overlooked by the college long after
my one-year Fellowship ended. Then came tighter financial times,
and the room was needed. We were offered two hours a week in
a room in the college, and there the group still meets to talk poetry
and other things every Tuesday night.

'Snow fell, undated', as Philip Larkin says, conjuring countless
centuries into the past with those few words. How moving they
are! How evocative of people long ago walking the unmade roads,
rising and going to bed in the dark, century after century. Marged
in her last, dark winter.

1947. I am nine and my sister is five. I am going out to play in the
snow. I don't want to take my sister with me but our mother makes
me. We live in Barry. We walk to Cold Knap Lake between five-

foot-high walls of snow. We try the ice. I make my sister go first as she's lighter. We walk out onto the ice. It cracks. A feeder stream has undermined the ice and my sister floats off on a frozen raft in a moment of terror before I manage to pull her to safety. It's my fault but I don't own up.

1962/3. The longest, coldest winter I remember begins on a freezing Christmas Eve. It is bitter cold, and above us is the clearest of starry skies as we step out of church after Midnight Mass. On Boxing Day it begins to snow. I am two and a half months pregnant, and watching my step. My daughter's second birthday is a month away. It snows until March, and our avenue in a Cardiff suburb lies snow-locked a hundred yards from the main road where the snow ploughs and the gritter lorries ply, and double-decker buses sail through a black mush of old snow towards town, libraries, shops. The depth and underlying slipperiness of the snow on the footpaths and the deep ruts of the frozen avenue keep me, the two year old and the pushchair locked in our castle of ice. At night 'the frost performs its secret ministry',[1] engraving the windows with ice-ferns on the inside. I wear fingerless gloves indoors. The pipes freeze.

1983/4. The car is buried in the drive at Cyncoed Avenue, Cardiff. The house has no central heating. We sleep with coats on the beds. We carry buckets of drifted snow out of the roof space to prevent it melting and dripping through the ceilings. Then we go and do the same for Mrs Morris next door.

2005. Peter B. and I, on a Poetry Live tour, bunk off from venue sandwiches and take the train to the next city, Sheffield, in time for a proper lunch. It begins to snow. Soon it is a blizzard. We sip Pinot Grigio and watch bubbles rising and snow falling beyond the glass walls of an arts centre restaurant. Ugly, serviceable concrete university buildings are veiled in falling snow. They rise from ground hallowed by snow. It is a scene of transfiguration. Peter and I, squiffy from sipping and snow-gazing, go our separate ways

---

1 Coleridge, 'Frost at Midnight'.

to nap in our warm rooms in the ugly multi-storey concrete hotel next door, where the water is hot and the darkening sky beautiful, and we can crash out until it is time to meet again for dinner. Part of me dreads being cut off somewhere on my travels, unable to get home for the weekend. Another part thrills at the luminous light, and watching the snow slowly fall, deepening by the day, stopping the world.

Home. Darkness. For a few precious hours the low sun travels just above the hedge and lights this room of glass. In the first weeks of January almost every day is clear. In the afternoon, before checking sheep, we leave the lights on, and as we turn for home we walk across the dark fields towards the lantern of a glowing house. Each day sunrise and sunset inch apart by minutes. Long, light evenings seem normal, short days like sickness. In the darkest days you can't believe in light.

Winter tames the sheep. They smell a freshly opened bale of hay, hear the rattle of a bucket, and come running. They follow us, butting and shoving with their woolly bodies, put their noses into our hands, sniff our pockets for gifts. They can read signals, just as Siani, our Welsh border collie, reads signs from our clothes. Which jacket? Which boots? Today is a boring day for Siani. On an office and study day she sees our clothes and turns away, flopping to sleep with a sigh, knowing we'll be at our desks all day. A jacket and boots tell her something exciting is about to happen. The best outings are those that allow her to help with the sheep. Sheep are her obsession. Not any sheep, just her own sheep. The sheep that graze all day in full view in Allt Maen's field on the other side of the hedge, yards from our garden, are of no interest. They are not 'her' sheep. Yet she will lie all day long with her nose under the gate of Cae Blaen Cwrt, watching her own flock.

Crows perch in the middle distance on invisible wires. Gulls flock over the fields following a tractor ploughing. Buzzards, and a pair of kites, watch out for carrion. Some nights the tawny owl calls, other nights the barn owl. The snowdrops are out, and thumbs and fingers of crocus and daffodil feel their way out of the dark.

Even in winter there is usually something in the garden for us to eat. Potatoes. A fist of leaves from the Cavolo Nero – an ever-lasting forest of Italian kale planted two years ago in the polytunnel. Leeks going to seed but still good. Beetroot. You can taste the earth in beetroot, and spinach, and other vegetables. Underlying the sweetness, however you cook it, is the shadow-taste of stone. It always seems like a miracle, that taste. It's the stone that made the soil we live on. We taste stone, and the minerals that made it, in the water that rises from the deep aquifer under the garden, the water we wash in, drink, water that bears minerals and metals into our blood and our bones. Jancis Robinson, wine expert, talks of the taste of wet stones in Chablis, and flint in Pouilly-Fumé and Sancerre. We are made of stone, metals, stardust.

Stardust. Five weeks of train journeys from mid-January to mid-February, visiting twenty-seven cities, performing thirty-three gigs to maybe fifty thousand GCSE students, makes me think of star-dust. This is because every pavement, path, pedestrian precinct, station platform, walkway, bridge, arcade, everywhere we walk in every town and every city in Britain, probably in the whole world, is starry with constellations of human spittle and gum. Gum-stars beneath our feet, and not a star visible in the city night sky, not Sirius, not Orion, not the Square of Pegasus, the Pleiades, the lovely planets, all so commonly seen in the dark of the country-side: Jupiter, that great lamp of winter nights. Every one of them lost from human sight in the glowing haze of street lights. When Comet Hale-Bopp was at its clearest in our night skies, my son phoned from Southampton for instructions on where to look for it. Standing in the garden with my mobile phone, I guided him, beginning with the constellation he knew best – Orion – and star by star led him to where the comet was. But he couldn't see it. It was lost in the orange haze of light pollution over the city. Yet that

night, here, far from street lights, my husband took the best photo-
graph he has ever taken, Hale-Bopp over our house, its tail a
whoosh of stilled flight against a sky of lapis lazuli blue.

Underfoot, wherever I travel, waiting for trains on my winter
tour with Poetry Live, I look down on pavement stars, spittle-
ghosts, dead stars spat out as the sea spits out shells. Above us, stars
so many light years away that their fires have long burnt out. It's
making me dizzy.

Home to a fall of snow. A white page.

Land

February

On the cusp between winter and spring. Mostly it's still indoor weather when I'm glad of bookish days. The afternoons are gaining light, a minute at a time, but there's no shine to the garden.

In mid-February, on a Friday night, the train sways slowly up the estuary into Carmarthen. My last winter journey of the season. I'm going home, and David is on the platform to meet me. My writing time can now begin in earnest. I feel exhilarated at the thought. Since Christmas I've been under pressure: deadlines loom for a final revision, another translation, a radio play. Then, time to walk the land again, to check the pregnant ewes – eight of them this year – to fill their racks with hay, to note buds and fists of growth breaking through branch and earth. Time to nourish creative energy with a second, deeper draught of those books I got for Christmas, among them Dannie Abse's memoir, the *Letters of Ted Hughes*, and John McGahern's stories, and a pile of old friends too.

Wellbeing. Being well. A well of being. An artist friend, Sandra, once said to me, 'You know how lovely it is when you're sitting by a window in a big chair and it's raining, and you have a book, and you think, "How lucky I am! How lucky!" That's a "found" poem.' Those with a talent for sudden, inexplicable joy will know exactly what Sandra meant. It describes being alive, having choice and chance and the gift of pleasure. It's about the solitary but not lonely individual relishing the simple fact of being, the pleasures of body and mind. Sight, sound and touch are explicit in that scene, and taste and smell are implicit since the rain, the window, the chair imply a familiar room, its privacy, possession and pleasures, perhaps a fresh brew of coffee, the smell of rain, a street outside, and a city. Sandra lives in London, so I know the last two details to be true. I lived many years in the city. Now that I live in the country, I look over a garden and fields to distant hills and far mountains. It's mild and there is for the first time a primrose light in the air. The snowdrops are out. Daffodil spears are coming up, yet the trees are still bare and the view is clear for miles. It is the sort of day when the single Welsh word *glas*, which means both blue and green, is just right, apt for the gradations of colour in hill country. The many tones of green of the close fields shift through blues and violets as the land rolls into the distance. *Glas*. That's it exactly.

I consider the significance of Sandra's and my framed views of outside worlds glimpsed from an interior or enclosure, from the stillness of a room, a garden. What's out there gives meaning to the safe place set and settled in its geography, its place on the planet. The beloved planet. I think of crushed houses, of smashed nests, of children's skulls as strong and delicate as egg-shell. Far away from the safe place, too far for *glas* to colour it right, other worlds racket in through the media's microphones. People tell their stories. The four walls of a building collapsed, the fallen roof, the broken city, the lost crushed in the dust or on their way to else-where. On the beloved planet cities fall apart, bridges are blown, roads are returned to rubble. 'Chaos is come again', and we humans have brought ourselves to this.

A big chair, a window, a book. Experience is mediated, modi-fied and deepened by literature. I've been reading Colm Tóibín's *The Master* all over again. The novel is based on the life of the novelist Henry James, but the imagining is all Tóibín's. He is wonderful on the pleasures of interiors, and of solitude. He tells how James wandered the cities of Europe, settling for periods in Rome, Florence, Venice, Paris, London, evading intimacy all his life. He shows how James turned away always at the last moment from emotional commitment, preferring the pleasures of solitude. Tóibín conjures the lovely interiors of apartments, villas, houses, in New England and in Europe, and in James's beloved Lamb House in Rye, where even the walled garden is a room. Tóibín gives us their lamplight, their rugs, books and paintings, the ampli-tude of their light and shade, their pleasing proportions. Sandra would recognise these enticements, and so do I. There's a side to all writers that loves nothing better than a book, a big chair, a window. Henry James knew, and surely Tóibín knows too, the pleasures of solitude and a life of literature. Tóibín's James seems to relish even his own melancholy. We witness his lost loves and passed-up chances, and see the pain of those from whom he turned away, as if reflected in the old mirrors of beautiful rented apartments. They continue to haunt the reader, and James, as the concluding paragraph of the novel demonstrates. James is home again from travelling:

> Lamb House was his again. He moved around it relishing the silence and the emptiness. He welcomed the Scot [his secretary] who was waiting for him to begin a day's work, but he needed more time alone first. He walked up and down the stairs, going into the rooms as though they too, in how they yielded to him, belonged to an unrecoverable past, and would join the room with the tasselled table cloths and the screens and the shadowed corners, and all the other rooms from whose windows he had observed the world, so that they could be remembered and captured and held.[1]

Yes! That, too, is it exactly.

Home from travelling, I relish this room, this house at the source, the *blaen*, source of my words and source of the stream, the Bwdram, that rises right here in the corner of the garden, a few metres from where I write these words. Long ago Marged, the previous inhabitant, drew all her water from that well. The water rises silently, pooling and then overflowing, no more than a gleam between ferns, to join the more copious waters of the spring in the field on the other side of the bank. That spring is intercepted below ground and water piped to our neighbour's farm a quarter of a mile downhill to the east at the bottom of the valley. Springs are potent symbols for creativity. Many writers have used the flowing of spring water, thawing from the ice or returning after drought, as a metaphor for the first flow of language coming again after a

---

1   Colm Tóibín, *The Master* (Picador, 2005).

period of writer's block. Hywel, our late neighbour, used to say, 'the water has come home'.

Until 1992 the land was not ours, and this room not built. At first we dreamed of owning just one small field. Cae Blaen Cwrt. It lay beyond a wired up gap in the hedge bank, a sunlit three-quarters of an acre glimpsed like the secret garden through the door in the wall. It had been part of the smallholding in Marged's day and shared our house name. Hywel sold it, with his farm, to a man from Buckinghamshire who bought it along with several other farms, and used his time, and grants, ripping out hedges, selling off farm buildings, ploughing the hill-country land too deeply and quarrelling with his neighbours. We offered him four thousand pounds for Cae Blaen Cwrt, four times its value, and over the months he said yes, then no, and we were alternately elated and disappointed. Then, in 1992, he went bankrupt, and the bank sold the lot to another neighbour, who knew we wanted the field. He offered it to us for the price he had paid. The land on this side of the valley was categorised as 'less favoured land' and our neighbour was happy to sell us eighteen acres. Much of it is steep, wooded, beautiful: a few fields, gorse-clad slopes, and the most beautiful bluebell wood we know. On New Year's Day 1993 we walked our land for the first time. In February 1994 we walked the fields to check our first eight Beulah Specklefaced ewes, took them hay, and waited nervously for their lambs to be born.

In the fifteen years since that day we have used no weedkiller or chemical fertiliser on the land. With the help of a tree expert friend, John Brooks, we restored the destroyed hedges and planted many more with native species. The hedges are dense now, making shelter for sheep and wild creatures, stopping the wind from blowing the skin off the land. In 2000 we planted an avenue of twenty-four hornbeams, groves and copses of native trees, now full of nests, the long grass beneath them alive with voles for the barn owl. Wild orchids appeared in Cae Blaen Cwrt that first spring, because it was no longer over-grazed. As the unfertilised grass got thinner, wild flowers increased, and countless butterflies appeared. As the young trees grew, the song thrush nested, and we heard it singing in our garden for the first time. It doesn't take much — just a bit of healthy neglect.

Later we dreamed an amplitude of space and light in a new room of glass and oak. The old longhouse is cosy and enclosed, with walls two feet thick. It was built to keep the weather out, not for views or light. The new room is an extension at the south end, opening from the extended old dairy turned kitchen and as spacious and light as we'd dreamed. It reflects the height and shape of the old house, a green oak frame double-glazed on two sides, the rest insulated with processed old newspapers, roofed with blue-grey slate from Penrhyn quarry in Gwynedd. The rain drains into a 'moat' running along the base of the two glazed walls, and over-flows into the Bwdram. Sun, moon, wind and rain send quivers of waterlight into the room.

I am eye to eye with the blackbird. She bustles, foraging on the ground. A kite flies low and slow over the field. Between the branches of the beech trees is a glimpse of our eight pregnant ewes, all descendants of our first little flock, grazing the top corner of the Fron. Sunlit reflections from the 'moat' run up the oak mullions between the glass. In rain the water sings and syncopates in the down-pipes. After dark the glass walls are glossy against the black of the night, and the glow from this room signals across the fields. One night after Christmas, they were feeding cattle at Pantycetris on the other side of the valley. That night all the houses were dark except for Blaen Cwrt. They liked seeing the lit house answering them across the fields. We like their lights too, signs of an occu-pied neighbourhood. I name the farms like a litany, and the field names too. Using them keeps them. I name and hold our five fields: Cae Blaen Cwrt, Cae Bach, Fron Blaen Cwrt, Fron Felen, Cae Delyn. Land.

There is something I can't quite put my finger on about the potency of place, placenames, their shades of meaning and the way we speak. It is as if they are entirely connected with the creative process, as if this place and its name, its meaning – 'source' – became the source of poetry for me. Was it working physically in the fresh air, the struggle to restore and create out of weather and wilderness and dereliction that set words going? It is a fact that I wrote my first published poems the year we bought Blaen Cwrt.

I take this up on a wild day, dark early under a heavy sky. Atlantic weather, the sky grey and flowing like the sea, whelming the land, the house, the slate over my head. This is no day to put away words and check the sheep – they'll be well hidden from the weather and their shepherd, sheltering in their gorse cloisters. The elm boards of this table – the top of a huge kitchen table found by David in an old hotel – glow in a circle of lamplight. Siani sleeps on the rug, the cats are curled by the Rayburn. Outside the rain is making a song-and-dance on sandstone and water, the gutters are doing their bullfrog gurgles and the wind rips the sky to rags. By next month I'll be out in the garden, but for now it's time for a book, a chair, for wellbeing, for this room with its wide view of land under the weather, and contained within me remain, as Colm Tóibín writes: 'all the other rooms from whose windows he had observed the world, so that they could be remembered and captured and held'.

February 2008. A sunny, silent, still day. David drags me away from work to walk the fields, preceded by Siani who gallops ahead, wriggling between the bars of the gates, and followed by Jac, meowing all the way, and our eight pregnant ewes in single file. A bizarre procession. David checks his fire of gorse branches, now a white circle with a tonsure of twigs. He rakes the twigs into the centre and it burns brightly. Daffodils are coming up in clumps in the ride. The hawthorn is 'coming into leaf / like something almost being said'.[2] There's frogspawn on the pond. The birds are singing.

Then days of sunlight, nights with ice-sharp stars, Sirius flashing green above the beech tree. Lyn from Blaen Cribor spots it and phones to ask its name. Today David calls me away from my computer for lunch. A surprise: he has laid it on the table on the terrace. I put on a fleece and sit at the table for the first time this year. The sun puts a warm hand between my shoulders. A kite flaunts elegantly overhead, red, white and black in sunlight. Then another. A pair.

2 Philip Larkin, 'The Trees', *High Windows* (Faber, 1974).

Breaking Waters

March

A thrush is singing. There was a time, when we first came here, when the song thrush never sang in our garden. The land to the west rises to a thousand feet. Our increasingly leafy eighteen acres lie in the lee of it. Some of our neighbours' fields are entirely tree-less, though the scars of old hedgerows are still visible in aerial photographs. In such exposed fields the prevailing winds from the west, and cold winds from the east, scour and sour the grazing, and there's not a scrap of shelter for the sheep. Before they saw the errors of their ways, the European grant-givers paid farmers to cut down hedgerows. Now the pressure is commercial. As the profits grow smaller, the machines grow bigger. Last year a contractor's harvesting machine on its way to a neighbour's huge barley field was way too wide for our lane. Its wheels straddled the tarmac leaving it untouched, gouging the narrow grass verges and crushing the banks of the open ditch which carries flood from the road in heavy rain. It ripped branches from our overhanging tunnel of trees – wild laburnum, cherry, rowan, elderflower, hawthorn – lofty enough for all normal loads and careful drivers of lorries, tankers, tractors and trailers to pass without difficulty, as occasion-ally they must, down our lane. The monster was not deterred, ripping its way through the arcade of trees, leaving ugly scars and torn branches.

A decade of tree and hedge planting since we bought and 'saved' our land has brought back the song thrush, the dragonfly, the early purple orchid, and many other flowers of the field. We planted an avenue of hornbeams leading between two fields, Cae Blaen Cwrt and Cae Bach, as a millennium gift to the planet. The avenue is flanked to its north-east by a new, sheltering hedge of mixed,

native species, and to the south-west by a grove of young trees. It
is now a place of dappled sunlight, birdsong and wild flowers. It's
a nursery for ewes with new lambs for a few weeks in spring. They
soon nibble it clean of old winter grass. We find sheep don't eat
the daffodils if there is enough grass beneath their hooves.

So, the song thrush. Once, a few years ago, we made a terrible
mistake. We burnt a pile of cut gorse too late in the season, and
must have scared the song thrush away from its nest of eggs,
because next day we found the nest, its eggs cold. Guilt and regret
shadowed us for weeks. Birdsong is not for our pleasure. It is the
sound of connection, of the link between bird and bird, bird and
nest, parent bird and nestlings. We benefit from the songbird's
presence. The thrush feeds on the snails that destroy the produce
in our garden. We must live with nature if we are to live at all.
Then, one evening this month a thrush sang again in the beech
brake at the end of Cae Blaen Cwrt. There is no evening song like
it. The thrush sings in rhyming couplets, the poet among birds, as
Browning knew: 'That's the wise thrush; he sings each song twice
over'.

I love the blackbird. It sings all day, every day, everywhere, pausing
only at nightfall. At dawn it is the first and clearest song. It does
not stop for rain. Indeed, it seems to love the rain, as if each drop
eased the song more fluidly, fluently from its throat. My daughter
emails from the city, from a terraced house with no front garden
at all, and only a tiny back yard which she has filled with greenery,
flowers and scents like a miniature Eden. 'What's this bird singing
all day?' she asks. She describes the song, a sweet repeated phrase
of four notes. It's a blackbird singing in the heart of the city, hidden
deep in a fig tree and overhanging lilacs in the garden back-to-
back with hers that nobody, thank goodness, has bothered to tidy
and tame. Perhaps, tonight, there is a blackbird singing in every
garden in Europe. It is, I think, the Muse.

Snow. Blossom on the blackthorn – the first petals on our leafless
hedges. A curdle of frogspawn in the pond; wool caught on old
brambles. Over it all a veil of snow that falls in the night, the fields

luminous under a three-quarter moon when we check the sheep. The rising sun soon melts most of it, leaving lacy intimacies on the north sides of hedge banks. Out of the sun it is cold enough for the remnants to lie crystallising all day. When they too melt, the grass will be glad of it after dry, frosty months. A sudden March downpour can't be absorbed by the frozen ground, and all turns to mud for a few days where the sheep wait at the gate each evening calling for their bucket of molasses and cereal.

The spring solstice. The breaking of waters. Legendary tides are expected on the Severn. River of superlatives, Britain's longest, pouring into the estuary to create the second highest rise and fall of the tide in the world. The source of the Severn is high on Pumlumon, the highest place in the mountains above Aberystwyth, though in truth it is less a peak, more a high, wet plateau. Up there two famous rivers are born, but when I walked there years ago the mountain offered me no sense of arrival. The reward lies in the thought of being at the source, the birthplace of the Severn and Wye. The Severn is born as a mud-puddle in soggy marshland, and finding the very place involves a slow squelch over tussocky ground, using tumps of old rush and cotton grass as stepping stones across hidden, boot-filling ditches. And even then you're not sure you are witnessing a birth.

The Severn flows east on a great meandering journey through the mountains of mid-Wales, then south along the Welsh-English border, gaining power and volume from every stream, folding waterfalls into itself as it goes, until it reaches the estuary and empties itself into the Bristol Channel. There, beyond the outpouring mouth of the Severn, is a momentous tide. Between low and high tide can be 14.5 metres. Not far off fifty feet! Awesome. Childhood memory brings me the Bristol Channel at Penarth in Glamorgan lapping the promenade in the morning, and by teatime the sea so far out I couldn't tell where the muddy, stony shore ended and the grey sea began.

The incoming tide, at its peak at the time of the spring solstice, rolling into the mouth of the Severn against the outpour of river water, reaches the narrowing throat of the river and piles up into a mighty wave that rolls up stream for twenty-five miles. The Severn Bore. This year a 1.5 metre Bore was reported – not the highest of Severn Bores, which can reach two metres – but a record was broken by a surfer who rode the Bore seven miles inland. To watch such a heave of water travelling so fast! To ride it between fields, past cathedrals. What a water-beast! What a muscular old mud-dragon of brown water! The physics of tide and moon, of the turning planet, the geography of mountain and river plain, the particular geology, the deepest of horseshoe bends and the right funnel shape for the tides to back up, the push and shove, the give and take of it, land shaping the Severn, the Severn shaping the land, have made it a wonder of nature. Even thinking about it is thrilling. I wrote 'The Flood Diary' in the winter floods of 2003, and recalled driving in a borrowed van through floods and, in the face of closed roads, taking a mountain track to get through. We saw a waterfall in the mountains of mid-Wales turned to a terrifying six-lane highway of hurtling water. We gasped. David said, 'Where is that going?' 'Shrewsbury,' I said. Sometimes poetry explains things better.

The Flood Diary

The weather girl reciting river names:
Severn, Wye, Humber, Aire and Ouse.
Atlantic lows lap at our living rooms,
the familiar map stormed by electric blues.
Out there where it's real the land is sodden,
the reservoir rocks at the lip of the dam.
Beasts stand as if stillness might rescue them,
islands of rooted cattle, ewes with their lambs.
We saw it coming – months of rain, and every
river taking to the road, the Severn
swollen on its way to Shrewsbury,
a ribbon of mountain water turned
to a six-lane torrent falling a thousand feet
with boulders, mud and branches in its throat.

We borrowed a van, and took the risk,
drove ninety miles through wind and rain north-east

to a timber yard in the hills for an oak truss,
by-passed the flooded Dyfi by forest track
and mountain pass. Strapped in, transaction over,
homebound in arrowing rain, we came upon
an old man knee-deep in a broken river
his car stalled in the current, its door held open
for the river to step in. We left it locked,
drove him to a neighbouring farm, shocked
but safe, and fled before the flood engulfed us too,
thought all the perilous way of its lights warning
till the battery ran out, or the river bore it away,
my hand on your thigh in silence, the barometer falling.

★

In a house in a southern English town
beside a modest river
used to collecting the slow
chalk Downland waters,

a grand piano paddles,
wades, treads water,
is lifted, riding the flood
in the room's harbour,

becomes an ark of rosewood
engulfed in filth, in the backwash
rainbows of petrol, diesel, drains,
its music under its wing.

A wave lifts the lid
on a gleam of ivory,
Its golden name wavers
underwater and is gone,

Bechstein,
an eel of light before
centuries of music drown
and the lights go out.

★

All winter, travelling by train,
the sodden length and breadth,
I ride above floodfields.
They built the lines high,
bridging hills and hollows
with embankments and viaducts.

Station after station
platforms flash with puddles.
A city gleams across the broken waters.
A cathedral grows reflective.
Horizons drown the sun,
its colours bleeding.

In the hotel, windows weep
and television brims.
We watch the news.
A city hold its breath
above the meniscus of a river
swollen with Pennine headwaters
and rising. They'll watch all night.

★

When the rains stop
and rivers empty into the sea,

there will be cities whose foothold
is dislodged a little,

fields that remember
becoming the sky,

the skull of a sheep filling
with tormentil and harebells,

and somewhere, among birdsong,
woodnotes and the strings of the wind,

the carcass and white teeth
of a piano.[1]

We wait for lambs. A friend asks: Do sheep feel pain when they give birth? What is labour pain for?

I have observed that they do, though they say nothing and make no fuss. The contractions of labour are a message, crucial to a safe delivery, and the ewe listens to her body. The ewe in labour moves away from the flock to seek a sheltered place on her own. She turns and turns on the spot, hoofing the ground as if making a bed. It's clear to me that this is pain with a purpose. It is a signal from a lighthouse to a ship to seek safe harbour. Why else would a cat make a nest in an airing cupboard, a mare take to the field's corner and wait, if she can, till there's no one around, or a ewe leave the flock and seek a safe place to lie down alone? Why else would a woman leave a party, go home, phone her midwife? The body has something overwhelmingly important to do, and the signals have to be powerful enough to ensure the message is clear. In labour, animals, human or beast, become all body. They are rivers of fierce sensation, and are all animal instinct. This pain is for the sake of the future.

We notice a ewe standing alone, in a corner, against a hedge, maybe. She does not come for her share of the bucket. We keep an eye on her. She scrapes the ground with a hoof, as if making a bed, turning as a cat does to shape it. She may lie down and lift her head straight up into the air as if straining. Soon the lamb is born 'in a syrupy flood', and the ewe, in what looks like a state of ecstasy, drinks the slippery strings of amniotic fluid from the ground, from the steaming coat of the lamb, sniffing and licking,

1 From *Making the Beds for the Dead* (Carcanet, 2004).

every sip, every breath of it crucial. It is hers, her own, her posses-
sion, and her bond with her lamb depends on it. The lamb sneezes,
shakes itself free, and tries to stand. It cries. The ewe finds a new
voice, like a soft growl, a new language for this new thing, and the
new, overwhelming obsession for the lamb she carried and did not
know she knew till this moment.

With a single heave, she gives birth to a second lamb, drinks it
too, licks with a flickering tongue, takes in its smell, counts her
two lambs and nudges each under her body for their first feed from
her teats, not yet milk, but colostrum, and the vital protection
against infection that will keep them alive. It is all to do with the
taste and smell of the fluids of her own body, which flowed out of
her with the lamb and which she licks and draws from its body in
strings, sometimes clear, sometimes yolky, until the lamb is clean,
and is hers, and they are bonded.

It is indeed a wonder. They are born in the field, in all weathers
– it's healthier that way. They often have twins, though never
identical, Beulah Specklefaced sheep, each one distinguished by
the particular black and white markings on its face. I recall one
first-timer giving birth in the stream. We had to dry the lamb with
a hairdryer. One icy moonlit midnight, when it was my turn to
go out and check, I tried to persuade a young ewe about to lamb
to come with me to the shed to a nice straw-filled pen. She
wouldn't have it. I waited, frozen stiff. Once her twin lambs were
safely born there was nothing for it but to leave them alone to give
them time to bond, and hope the fox kept away. In the frozen
early hours David came with me to check, and all was well.
Holding one crying lamb each, walking backwards all the way with
the ewe dancing between us licking first one lamb then the other,
we lured her into the barn to a long draught of water, a bucket of
feed, fresh hay, and safety. The Beulahs rarely need help in giving
birth, but once or twice over the years I have helped a ewe deliver
its lamb, freed its head from a tight collar of skin, taken the head
in one hand, two front hooves in the other and pulled at the next
contraction. Or I've pushed the lamb back a little to bring out both
hooves together. Something gives, and it's born in a rush. Then I
am heady with joy and the ewe is in ecstasy. No one ever taught
me to do this. Books help, but in the end it is just animal instinct.

The lambs have no fear of Siani, and come to the gate to touch noses with her. She finds their impertinent intimacy disconcerting. She doesn't move or make a sound. She seems to hold her breath until, suddenly, they turn and gallop off, a rampage of lambs, like children ringing the doorbell and running away. Perhaps the scent of her on the land keeps the fox at bay. We have only lost one lamb to the fox, when a late-birthing ewe had her lamb far from the house, above the oak wood where there are certainly fox-holes. We should have brought her in at once, not waiting for evening. By the time we realised the lamb was not there, she was calling and calling, the sound of hopelessness. Within a day she had forgotten, and was grazing quietly with the flock as if grief had never happened.

A Spring Heatwave

April

Once, as March turns to April, Dylan brings the children for a few days. In New Quay they watch the dolphins wheel through the waters within the arm of the harbour. There are 127 bottlenose dolphins in the Cardigan Bay family. How on earth – or at sea – do they count dolphins? Counting sheep is hard enough. As there are only two resident dolphin families off the British coast, we're lucky to have them. The children return full of excitement. Once, years ago, downhearted at a difficult work time, David and I, too early for a dinner date with friends in Aberystwyth, strolled on the promenade for half an hour. A red sun was setting into the sea, and in the path it made between itself and where we stood on the shore, a pod of dolphins began to leap, over and over, high, right out of the water, in a spotlit performance so dazzling that all our anxiety was burnt up in the glory. As Annie Dillard says in *A Pilgrim at Tinker Creek*: 'all a poet can do is be there'.

2007. Warm, dry March days become an April heatwave. It reaches almost 30 degrees. Every day, lunch on the terrace. The sandstone slabs hold the sun's heat long into the evening. Siani and the cats luxuriate in the sun. Six weeks without a drop of rain. We didn't put a ram with the sheep until November, so this year the lambs are late. The pregnant ewes lie panting under the grove of trees to the west of the hornbeam ride. We consider the possibility of a vineyard on Fron Blaen Cwrt. In the weather's present tense April heat feels like forever and ever. We enjoy the thoughtless happiness that warmth and sunlight bring, caught too by the warning it carries. This is not normal. Nothing can be depended on any more, not the winds of March, nor April showers. The climate is unweaving the poetry.

One ewe shows signs of a prolapsed uterus, and we consult our young neighbour, Gethin. He fixes a 'spoon' under the sheep's tail, a plastic device with loops which he fixes into place and ties with strands of her fleece, warning us it may not work. David had a bad experience a few years ago, when he found a pregnant ewe with a prolapse and took her to the vet, where she died at the surgery, along with twin lambs which were not ready to be born. It was very distressing, and he doesn't want to see such a thing again. For a few days this ewe is fine. Then the 'spoon' comes loose, and the prolapse bulges. We call the vet. He is young, his name is Nathan and he's Dutch. He tell us that he doesn't like the spoon system as it risks injuring the uterus. He gives us a harness, a businesslike contraption made of strips of red fabric like safety belt material, with plastic buckles. He shows us how to strap it on. It sits comfortably around her, her legs in the loops, the straps buckled on her back, the uterus kept firmly in place by a rectangle of fabric that still allows her to pee and defecate. We are under instruction to watch her carefully, and to make sure we are with her when she goes into labour.

David is full of foreboding. As the weather is hot I take a chair and a book, and spend the day close to her pen in the field. Nothing happens. At night David goes out twice to see her, and I go at six in the morning, and watch her whenever I can during the day. The other ewes lie panting in the shade of the hornbeam ride. One by one they all lamb without trouble, and the lambs are up and playing, safe and cool in the long grass under the trees. The only one left is the ewe with the prolapse. We've watched her for a week and we're tired. Another hot day, and she's restless. I let her out of the pen and she takes to the hollow close to the hedge bank, a sign that she is going into labour at last. David is a prophet of doom, 'I don't know what's in there but I don't like it.' 'Lambs,' I say, 'Twins I expect. Don't worry. Once the waters break the pressure will be off and I'll remove the harness. She'll be fine.' He goes into his office. The ewe turns round and round on the spot and hoofs the ground. I take a closer look – she's wet, there is no sign of the prolapse, her waters have broken, so I undo the buckles of the harness, and sit on the grass close to her, watching. Within half an hour she gives birth to the first lamb without a scrap of trouble. Twenty minutes later the twin arrives. She licks them with what looks like adoration, and nudges them to suckle. She is in charge now, and we can sleep tonight.

'I told you so,' I said when David came out to admire the ewe fussing over her new lambs, 'talking' to them in a low growl.

I'm thinking about sandstone, walking on the terrace on these warm April days, and reading about stone, amazed all over again to be reminded that, apart from water, what wears stone away is wind. The world's winds flowing over hills and hollows, rasping at rock, licking islands and continents, scraping the finest layer of dust from one place and depositing it in another. Hither and thither over the world go its shifting molecules. So every day the mountains lose a skin. Every day they are both less and more. Topsoil is scraped from plough-land, deserts scoured, rock honed to sharpness. What an exfoliation!

This reminds me of a wonder I heard the late-night radio weatherman tell his listeners one unseasonably warm spring night years ago: that hot, dust-bearing winds from Africa were sweeping Britain, and a red dust had been noticed on cars. I went outside with a cloth and swiped the bonnet of the car, then brought it into the light. It was stained with what looked like a rust-red pollen. Saharan dust! Spring, and the swallows will soon be back from the south to nest and raise their young in the lofty roof of our barn. Birds and stone-dust riding the hot wind from Africa. A bird with a grain of Saharan sand in its feathers. The spring night is suddenly electric with a sense that our planet is intimate and knowable, shivering in its skin, shedding that skin to the wind. Technology has given the earth the means to tell us what it has always known.

Two things set me on this stony path: walking barefoot on the warm sandstones of the terrace, and writing about Pentre Ifan. I've known the megalith all my life, since early childhood days spent in Pembrokeshire with Ga on the farm. It's a massive but elegant cromlech in a field in the hills overlooking the Irish Sea, about an

hour from here. It's a pictogram from the alphabet of stone. I read
its silhouette as the very word for cromlech. The stones come from
Carn Meini, an outcrop of igneous granite as old and as hard as
any rock on the planet, an outburst of molten dolerite and rhyo-
lite from the earth's mantle. Under Carn Meini the fields slip
downhill to the sea, the underlying sedimentary rock blown away
in the wind, aeon by aeon, from its bony shoulders.

A new word. Orogeny: that which happens in a period of moun-
tain formation. The cunning Araucaria, King of the *Guardian*
crossword setters, devised this clue:

'Gold I return to American city for mountain building'. 7
letters.

First 'or' (gold), then 'ego' (backwards), and finally 'New York'.
Mountain building. Orogeny. Orogenesis. (Greek. Oros: moun-
tain + genesis: creation.)
    It is strange how often a word arises from nowhere to meet a
current preoccupation, and how likely it is that it will outcrop
again somewhere soon.

April 2007. The swallows arrive. It is still so hot that they must
think it's Africa. It's the very pair, we assume, that nested here last
year, raising three broods of young on the same beam in our barn.
Now they are back. There they are, one early April day, trying the
air above the garden and Cae Blaen Cwrt for familiar places and
perches. They settle for a while on their old favourite, the top
branch of the weeping birch by the pond in the field. Then, after
much aerial preambling, they slide their low-flying jet shapes
through the gap over the big barn doors, like Harriers daring the
deep valleys between mountains.
    Last year Jac caught one young fledgling from the third and final
brood. It had just learnt to fly. Jac snatched it from the air as David
rushed to open the big doors so that the young bird might see its
way out. A black cat, his mouth full of inky blue black feathers.

After watching the parent birds successfully rear three broods, it was a terrible sight. This year the cats have new rules: in spring and summer the barn doors are kept shut, the catflap locked to keep them out. The cats' winter night quarters in the hay are banned in the breeding season. There are kennels, little sheds and a poly-tunnel where they must seek their shelter now.

Songbirds all over Britain are being killed at such an unprecedented rate by cats and grey squirrels that their numbers are in serious decline, so warns a survey just published. Domestic cats usually bring their kill home to consume or abandon on the doorstep or the kitchen floor, so we know our cats' prey. Although occasionally young birds are brought – a robin, once a redstart, another time a snipe – it happens rarely. Our cats prefer fur to feathers: mice, voles, sometimes a rat, a weasel, and many rabbits appear on the step. We are grateful to our cats for keeping rabbits from our vegetable garden and the house free from vermin. One day we were having tea on the terrace when Siwan, our shyest, wildest cat, brought one by one a brood of newborn mice, squeaking, hairless, pink, the size of sugared almonds, and ate each one of them with a single gulp. Years ago, after seeing a rat in the roof space, we put Jac there. He killed it in five minutes. In his youth young rabbits were Jac's main prey, at the height of his powers one a day. Nothing pleased him better than fresh rabbit. He killed it quickly, and ate it bones and all, leaving nothing but the gut. Sometimes he would eat his fill and disappear to sleep it off for twenty four hours, leaving the 'trousers' for the other two cats. This is typical wild cat behaviour. Lions, tigers eat all they can when they can, because tomorrow they may eat nothing at all. This kill is natural, and seems fair. The cat kills to eat. Jac is a very big cat, lean and muscular, half-Siamese, half farm cat. His Siamese genes give him muscular strength, great size and the instinct and ability to catch and kill prey almost as big as himself. In his heyday, he wasted nothing of his kill. I respect Jac for it. There is a belief among some Native American tribes that if you hunt you must use every single part of the animal you kill, wasting not a feather, not a pelt, not a bone. They believe this respects the animal and reveres its life, teaching us how to live with life and death.

Bluebells. *Endymion non-scriptus*. One of the reasons I longed to
own the land was the bluebell wood. Two and a half acres of sessile
oaks which in April seem to be standing in blue water. The wood,
on a steep south-facing slope, is probably an ancient patch of
woodland that has been coppiced many times over centuries. In
the early 1970s we were welcome to walk there, but when our
neighbour, Hywel, sold the farm and the land, the new man was
a very different landowner. We watched hedges on other parts of
the land being torn up, and we feared for the wood. We saw
schemes tried and failed, neighbours offended, animals in a bad
way. It was a rule of terror, and we dared not set foot on the land.
We could only gaze into the bluebell wood from the lane that runs
along the valley bottom. Aprils came and went. When our volatile
neighbour went bankrupt in 1992, and the eighteen acres (five
fields and the bluebell wood) were ours, we could walk the land
again.

That April, 1993, was a superb bluebell year. Early winter rain
and cool spring sunlight through leafless oak trees brought one of
the finest flowerings ever. The fact that they were ours, and while
we were in charge no one would ever, ever plough them up, made
theirs the bluest blue in the world, the almost violet of the dress in
Renoir's *La Parisienne* in the National Museum in Cardiff, lapis
lazuli blue, rarest of pigments. And the smell! We walked the
coconut-scented gorse track to where the yellow gorse to the left
gave out and the blue floor of the wood was spread before us, the
scent changing from spice to floral. We were dizzy with breathing
it. Ours!

April 2007. We walk the golden gorse track, and every day we see
the blue of the wood intensify. But this year it doesn't quite
happen. It's too hot, too dry, and there is no single moment when
we say: this is it, the bluebell wood at its peak. One day it's nearly
there. Next day perhaps not, and each day thereafter the blue and
the scent have faded a little.

This is the point of course. The native British bluebell is bluer and more prolific and more gorgeous in Britain than anywhere else on earth because of our maritime island climate, because of mild winters, because of our rain. It is not the American bluebell, which is a campanula, a different flower entirely, not the Spanish bluebell, which is a larger, paler, less delicate relative which lacks the drooping head. Our native bluebell is unknown on earth except in lands beside the Atlantic, and here it flowers best of all. Will Endymion be lost to climate change?

So April turns to May, leaving a fading scent and colour, a slight sense of loss, of regret, of change. I wake dreaming of rain.

In Oradour

May

May 2007. There is always a blackbird – always a pair of black-birds: the male to sing all day long from the first sign of spring until the end of June, and the female to busy herself all winter shopping in the mulch on the ground under the bird feeders, or beside me in the polytunnel once her brood is reared. I like to think that this bird is the eternal blackbird, the one which has kept me company here for over twenty years. The one blackbird which has sung from its perch in an ash tree, and fed every winter since blackbirds were first recorded in Irish and Welsh poetry, the blackbird in the poetry of the early bards and the manuscripts of the scribes. But this black-bird is like no other. She wears a white collar, white cheek patches and a white cap. She looks rather prim. A nursemaid. Last spring we worried that her strange appearance would put off a mate, and that she might be rejected by the other blackbirds. However, she had a fine mate, black and glossy, and they nested in the hedge by the lane and reared a clutch of young. Right now she picks and tosses aside the mulch as if rummaging for bargains at a sale.

May 2004, France. The blackbird's is the only voice heard in Oradour-sur-Glane, a village near Limoges, in the Limousin. In the village streets there are people strolling, but no one speaks, or smiles, or acknowledges another. The small sign we pass at the gates to the village reads *Silence*. We need no such prompt. Ahead the street takes an elegant curve into sunlight, as in most French villages. But in Oradour the houses gape, roofless, windowless, like skulls in a charnel house. Every terraced house, detached house, the *mairie*, Post Office, three schools, a surgery, several dressmakers, cafés, hotel, bar, grocer, butcher, baker, farrier, ironmonger, garage, the great medieval church, these and all that had served the village, flanking the street ahead and all adjacent streets between lost gardens and rows of sweet chestnuts, were torched by an occupying SS division of the German army on 10 June 1944. First all citizens were ordered to assemble in the village square. There they were separated into groups and herded into Oradour's larger buildings, women and children into the church, men and boys into several barns. Then the soldiers shot the men and fired the barns. Five boys and young men escaped.

In the church, the herded women must have heard the commotion. One woman, Mme Rouffanche, survived by jumping through the glass of the great window behind the altar and pretending to be dead. She is the only witness to what happened in the church. A few soldiers placed 'a box... from which hung strings which trailed the ground' close to the nave. It exploded, filling the church with smoke. The women rushed into a side chapel. The soldiers fired a volley of shots into them, then piled straw and wood around them, dead and alive, and set fire to it.

Connections. June 1944. I am seven. It is two days after my birthday. I remember it well, remember my presents, the antique teaset from Ga, my grandmother, the new dress my mother made with red and blue taffeta bought with all the clothing coupons she and the family could muster. There isn't much to buy for birthdays in the shops, so we children are given precious things, though we hardly know it. My father has found a French musical box in a junk shop. Beautiful, its oak lid inlaid with mother of pearl scrolls and a little ship. I love it. I will keep it forever. I have it still, and the teaset. They are here, in my study. Treasures.

While I romp on Ga's bed and race about the house, over-excited by birthday joy, the forces of good and evil are mustering elsewhere. A terrible violence and unimaginable cruelty lie days away. I know, even on my seventh birthday, that 'there is a war on'. That's what they say after every command to eat my greens, turn the lights off, don't waste good food, don't complain, be thankful. I more or less follow the rules, but I don't know what war means, except that my mother's friend Ena comes to our house to cry a lot. Her husband was a pilot in the RAF, and he's been killed. He was 'a hero', they say. Also, just along the coast from our house in Barry, near Cardiff, the Germans drop a bomb on the harbour. There's a hole in our dining room window made by a piece of shrapnel. Sometimes I have to sleep under the stairs, or with my mother and baby sister under a shelter like a metal table. Mostly Ga and I are safe a hundred miles away, at Fforest Farm, in Pembrokeshire, but for my seventh birthday we're all together in Barry.

Spring 2004. My husband and I drive south from the ferry port of Cherbourg through the towns of northern France. There are flags everywhere, the French flag, the Union flag, and the Stars and Stripes. They are preparing for their D Day sixtieth anniversary celebrations. Suddenly, I remember something, and for the first time understand its significance. It is a revelation. A curtain is drawn back and everything flooded in light. For the first time I can date a puzzling childhood memory.

June 1944. It's a few days before my birthday and I am counting the days, trying on a new dress while it is still full of pins, and all the excitement and the long light evenings make me too jumpy to sleep in spite of blackout curtains. I sleep at last, and my father comes into my bedroom and wakes me. He lifts me onto the windowsill, pulls back the curtains and points into the night sky over Cold Knap Lake, the houses and the park. 'Look,' he says. 'I don't want you to miss this.' The sky is full of aeroplanes. Lights. A roar of continuous sound like the after-hum when I bang the low notes on the piano. Hundreds of planes from RAF St Athan in Glamorgan, and from elsewhere too, flying south over Barry, the Bristol Channel, and, I now believe, across the English Channel to France.

That must have been the early hours of D Day, the day of the all-out push to liberate France. How does memory suddenly make sense of itself sixty years after the event? I know now that my father had wind of something being planned in Britain. As a BBC broadcasting engineer his work was considered part of the war effort, so he was not called up for military service. BBC employees were in a unique position to sniff the wind for signs of the way the war was going.

May 2004. Oradour in early summer. The ruins are a monument, masonry and metal making a shape of the past, timbers burnt, roofs and upper floors fallen. Remaining in every house is what fire could not burn and no enemy soldier looted: iron bedsteads, Singer sewing machines, bicycles, metal wine racks, pumps, sundry machines, cars burnt in their garages, We know the names of the dead: M. Avril, Mme Reignier, J. Rouny, Doctors Paul and Jacques Desourteaux, father and son... and so on, and on. We know their work, their trade, their professions. Seamstress, glovemaker, dentist, doctor, teacher, butcher, baker, hotelier, and all the others who made up the community of a perfectly ordinary village.

While my mother stitched into the night on her Singer sewing machine, making my taffeta party dress, the regional commander of the SS, the first regiment, der Führer, of Das Reich division, was planning the destruction of Oradour. Two days after my seventh birthday, on 10 June, all its citizens were slaughtered. Among them were my contemporaries, seven-year-old children ushered with their teacher from their schools by the soldiers. For three of the girls, it was their birthday week too. For one, Michèle Vauchamp, her birthday was to be her death day.

We walk in silent Oradour, listening to the blackbird's orisons. The church is a beautiful ruin, the flagstones of its floor laid unevenly like a shore from which seas and centuries have receded. The bell lies where it fell under the tower, tortured by fire into a huge, deformed lump, its tongue welded into its throat, vestiges of the words once engraved about its rim still legible, but senseless. They cut out its tongue. They put language to the torch. In a side aisle stands the confessional, a survivor, sheltered under a part of the church that is roofed with stone. The bodies of two children were found inside it. It keeps its secrets, the complexities of love, courage, betrayal, loss, grief, goodness and greed that go on anywhere where we are human. One day, a sin confessed. Next day, it's all over.

In the car on the way back to our home for a week in a Limousin
farmhouse, conversation gradually returns, though sombrely. All
who see such things must understand why the European dream is
so much more valued by those whose experience of war was this.
We had never heard of the atrocity of Oradour-sur-Glane. Most
people haven't. Everyone should know what happened there.

Auburn Limousin cattle lie flicking their tails in deep grass over
the auburn soil of the fields. Further south limestone-pale Charo-
lais graze on limestone terrain. The weekly markets sell the
produce of the fields all around us. The wine carries a hint of the
taste of the very rock beneath our feet. The glory of what's local,
and continuous, and part of a culture that is deep and ancient and
human.

The end of May. Hay-on-Wye Festival of Literature time, where
the blackbird is still singing, A few years ago in Hay it sang all of
a rainy day till dark, and again from three the following morning.
I know because I was commissioned to spend from noon one day
until dawn the next day sitting in Salem Chapel writing a poem in
response to a non-stop live performance of Erik Satie's *Vexations*.
Composed of eighteen notes repeated over and over for eighteen
hours, it was played by a team of many pianists, amateur and
professional. Making way for each other, the pianists smoothly
exchanged first their left, then their right hands, with never a lost
note. I got sleepy and cold, but not bored. Hearing the piano
repeating its notes was no more boring than listening to the sea
break on the shore, or the blackbird's four-note song sung over
and over.

Towards midnight a team from BBC Radio 3 arrived to set up
their broadcasting equipment in the chapel, and to record me and
my fellow poet, Owen Sheers, reading our brand new poems. From
midnight until 6 a.m. the performance of Satie's piece was broad-
cast live on Radio 3 to the world's insomniacs. My poem, 'Erik
Satie and the Blackbird', was scheduled for the early hours, and at
break of dawn, the blackbird began to sing. The ever-inventive
Radio 3 team took a microphone out and recorded the birdsong,

so that the poem could be heard accompanied by the very black-
bird which was the presiding muse of the poem.

> The blackbird sings
> for eighteen hours
> with a bead of rain
> in its throat.
> First notes at first light.
> Four in the morning
> and he'll be there
> with his mouth full of gold.
>
> The piano crosses an ocean
> on one wing,
> noon to midnight
> and through to dawn.
> This is the nightshift.
> You and the rain
> and the pianist awake,
> navigating the small hours.
>
> While the blackbird sleeps
> under a dark wing,
> the town breathing,
> the wash of a car on a wet street,
> the world turns over
> in the dark. The sleepless
> travel on. They know by heart
> their own refrains.
>
> The pianist doesn't turn the page.
> Just back to the top
> where music collects
> opening its throat to the rain,
> and somewhere two bells
> count down the hours
> towards first light, landfall,
> the downpour of a blackbird singing.[1]

1 From *Making the Beds for the Dead* (Carcanet, 2004).

Islands

June

I know my favourite island by its old Welsh name: Enlli – *ynys yn y lli*, island in the current. It's a beautiful name. The waters of the Irish Sea utter it on the shore as they have for millennia, for eras, ages, chrons. Repeat the phoneme slowly, *ll-ll-ll*.[1] The sound breaks on the ear as waves on a beach. Could the sound of breaking waves be the source of this Welsh fricative? Bardsey, the island's Norse name, adds another chapter to the story, but it is unmelodious to my ears, and omits history's Dark Ages and the legends of the place. Give me any day the soft mutation of waves on the shore at Enlli, ynys yn y lli, island in the current.

My first island was not really an island at all. Sully Island probably takes its name from Old Norse *súla*, a gannet. It lies sometimes offshore, sometimes joined to the shore at Lavernock. (Is Lavernock Welsh, Llan Brynach, perhaps, the church of Brynach? But I'm just guessing now.) Just a few acres of rabbit-nibbled heath, Sully Island rises from the littoral at the edge of the Bristol Channel in the county of Glamorgan. At low tide you can walk to it across a rocky causeway, a spine emerging from the sea like stepping-stones above the rock pools, mud, sand and draining waters of the Channel. When the tide is out, if you're ten or eleven years old and it's summer and you and a friend have bread, cheese, apples and a bottle of pop, the island is irresistible. Easy to drop your bike above the beach, cross the causeway and allow yourself to be accidentally marooned. You'll tell your mother the tide came in when

---

1 The sixteenth sound of the Welsh alphabet.

you weren't looking. You are surrounded by the rising sea, the second greatest rise and fall of the tide in the world, and your heart is high with the thrill of it. Marooned! On the southern, far side of the island, nothing but the sea glittering and stretchmarked by perilous currents as far as the mist-green hills of Somerset, Gwlad yr Hâf, the summer country. Nothing to break the sea but the blink of the Breaksea lightship and its two-note moan on foggy nights as you lie in your bed at the top of a tall house in Penarth. Nothing else lies between you and England but the islands of Flatholm and Steepholm, the one flat, the other steep, with their Old English name, *holm*, for island. Tough luck if the weather should turn, clouds darkening the grey-green waters of the open sea, and a cold rain-laden wind should breathe in from the western approaches. Your shorts, daps and spare jumper are no protection, and there is no sheltering tree. You are living an adventure story. At first it's thrilling. As you get colder you long for dry land and the sea takes an eternity to let you go.

Midsummer 2000. I am spending a week on Enlli as Poet in Residence. David comes too. As instructed, we have brought clothes for every kind of weather, and enough food for two weeks lest rough seas delay our return. The passage between the island and the mainland is treacherous, and there are days even in summer when the regular boat from Pwllheli cannot cross the sound. We are on the slipway at Porth Meudwy near Aberdaron early on a warm summer morning to wait for the boat. Seven sixth form art students and their teacher from Coleg Dwyfor wait with us, and my host from the Bardsey Trust is there to welcome us.

From the mainland Enlli is a humpback whale, five hundred feet of rock rising from the sea, the north side of the mountain, Mynydd Enlli. To qualify for mountainhood the summit needs to reach a thousand feet, but the north face rising sheer from the sea and the steep bracken slopes on the far side make Mynydd Enlli feel as mountain-like as many a landlocked peak. To the south, hidden from the mainland, lie sunny, stone-walled fields, farm, chapel, old school and clusters of dwellings. Among them is Rhedynogoch, where our friends, the poet Christine Evans and her husband Ernest Evans live, and Tŷ Pellaf next door, Ernest's old home. Ernest, lobster fisherman, part-time lighthouseman and

bearer of the post and goods from the mainland, was the last baby
born on the island. He and Christine live on Enlli for six months
of the year, returning to the mainland for the winter. Our stay is
made immeasurably more delightful, comfortable and civilised by
the presence of these good friends. Christine is on the slipway as
we disembark, to welcome us and take us to our quarters in the
lighthouse, about half a mile away. Our luggage will follow by
tractor.

The lighthouse is a privileged place, the only building on the
island to have a flush toilet and, when the generator works, elec-
tricity. Like all Britain's lighthouses, it is run by Trinity House,
and is now automatic.

A first evening walk from the lighthouse to the tip of the head-
land. We watch waves break on the rocks below. Every sixth wave
is huge, gathering force to fall streaming into whiteness with the
sun shining through its molten streams. Seals hang in the sea,
watching us. Riding the big power of the evening sea they are
shadows in green amber, green glass. A few weeks short of
midsummer, the sun is still red above the horizon. We gaze west
across the sea towards Ireland. Enlli is closer to Dublin than to
Bangor, and Christine tells me the loom of Dublin can often be
seen across the sea. Flowers lie low here, keeping their heads
down, thrift, blue squill, birdsfoot trefoil, tormentil. Above the sea,
on the rocks, lies a dead ewe.

There are no rabbits on the island, no rats, no cats, badgers, foxes
or weasels, no predatory mammals, and visitors are not allowed to
bring dogs. Nesting birds are safe here, except for those vulnerable
to gulls.

Enlli is sanctuary and breeding ground to huge numbers of
Manx shearwaters, which spend all daylight hours flying just above
the sea, so close that they shear the waves. The oldest wild bird
ever recorded is a Manx shearwater. It was ringed in 1953, as an
adult, at least five years old, and ringed again in 2003, at least fifty-
five years old. Their feet are not evolved to perch, walk or land
on earth. They nest in burrows, and would be vulnerable were
there rats or weasels on the island. Only when darkness falls do
they come home to rest. Then they fold their wings and arrow
into the relative safety of the burrows.

The wind picks up bringing a fine, drenching rain off the sea.

We come in to change, open wine, make supper. We share the lighthouse kitchen with Artist in Residence Paul Lewin, who paints fine land- and seascapes. Paul has been here for a month. He has baked bread. We cook together, sharing our wine and his good bread.

The rain passes, and darkness falls, so we wrap up warm to go out to watch the shearwaters return from the sea. An angelic host, a choir of cries, each bird a flash in the intermittent beam of the lighthouse. It's hard not to cry out at each spark as if watching a whoosh of fireworks. Each bird flares and is doused by the dark as the lighthouse beam swings away over the sea. Their screams ring the night.

We're cold from standing still. Home to make up a bed, fill hot water bottles and nest for the night. The day was hot, but it's cold now. The generator is not working, so there's no hot water. We light oil lamps and candles. There is a breath of damp air in the ground-floor bedroom and in the unaired bed. Cold seeps through the single glass of the window. Though it's midsummer we are so close to the sea and its mists that we're glad to borrow warmth from each other, and the hot water bottles.

Sunday morning, 11 June. We sit in the sun on a cushion of close-grazed turf scattered with thrift and dry sheep droppings, listening to the cries of oystercatchers and the psalm of the seals. The wind across the labyrinth of my ear is small, feathery. A skylark. The quiet wash of the sea. The singing of seals. Dei the shepherd, who lives next door to Christine and Ernest, drives past in the tractor on the track to the lighthouse. David reports the dead ewe we found below the headland. Dei goes to inspect the ewe, diagnoses a broken neck from a fall from the cliff, and tosses the sheep into the sea to be swallowed and dismantled, dispersed in the salty waters among thousands of years of human and animal bones, to become sand, to begin again.

A day of seals. We're used to the grey Atlantic seal in Ceredigion, seal pups on the beaches in September, a black head watching from the waters. But I've never seen seals on shore in such great numbers as on Enlli. Over three hundred come in every morning to bask on rocks at Henllwyn Bay like so many Naked Majas. Seal songs. Low calls like the soft growl of a ewe talking to a lamb. High complaints like chained dogs. As they spread their flippers light glows through their webs. They stretch and roll over heavily, disturbing each other, and the sound rises and gathers to a crescendo following the wave of movement. Occasionally there's a snarl or a low, musical roar as a bull heaves among them. Then, suddenly, after an hour or so, there they go! Off to graze the kelp in the shallow waters of the littoral. What a commotion of slip-shod slithering! Their heads on the surface turn shoreward, watching us. About a hundred seals remain. Some, dry after lying in the warm air, fold their flippers like suede gloves. We have been watching for hours. There is no end to their fascination. So much variation of colour, tone, marking. Some are black, some blond, many speckled as oystercatcher eggs, none really grey. Now their singing is soft as wind over ship's rigging. There is more rolling in their bodies today than there is in the waters of the sea.

Later we walk from the lighthouse past Henllwyn Bay, then across to Porth Solfach, and north along the west coast of the island, following the path above low cliffs and rocky edges, with oystercatchers kicking up a fuss all the way. We come upon the north-west bird hide, a wonderful little hermit's hut of driftwood and pebbles, weighted with stones lashed down with sea-rope. It has a bench about six feet long with a surprisingly dry foam mattress, and a plank to unhook and lift at eye level. I love it. What a writer's hut it would make! Now that we are invisible the oyster-catchers fall silent. A few feet away a small brown bird feeds a fat fledgling with insects. Brown, speckled like a thrush. A rock pipit.

The path runs out at the side of Mynydd Enlli where it falls sheer to the sea. We strike straight up the mountain through bracken and heather and halfway up meet three excited birdwatchers who reckon they've seen a sub-alpine warbler. Five hundred feet up in the sunshine at the summit, a silver sea lies all around us. We spot a man on a ledge, and worry until we see he is using a mobile phone – the only place on Enlli reached by Orange! Home down the rough slopes, along the coast to the boathouse, to Cafn, and Henllwyn, and along the neck of the island to the lighthouse.

Ben – our other lighthouse lodger, a natural scientist – brings a strange dead fish to identify. A sea-hen, or lumpsucker. *Cyclopterus lumpus.* I think of Christine's poem, 'Encounter', where the fisherman (Ernest?) finds a lumpfish floating on the sea, hauls it on board, and 'sits it doll-like on the hauler box'. He watches it, 'adjusting / like an old man coming startled from a drowse / in his own house'. Then,

> Gently he lowers it to the water
> and watches as slowly, purposefully
> the lumpsucker sinks
> deliberately down, into the dark.
> The sounder here shows fifteen fathoms.[2]

In a rock pool I find a vivid blue creature caught in the weed. It looks like a strange sea anemone, but the book suggests:

Vellella vellella, By-the-wind-sailor. A modified siphonophone with a bluish disc reaching 8 cm. in diameter which encloses the float and contains a horny skeleton equipped by a sail. Habitat, pelagic, surface-dweller. Distribution, Mediterranean, and Atlantic.

Could it be a By-the-wind-sailor, blown way off track by storm and climate change? I hope so. I love the name and welcome it into my journal.

12 June. An extraordinary night. Sea fog envelops the island. We're tired and in bed by 11 o'clock, reading, shutters closed against the repeated five flashes of the lamp. Suddenly, deafening, right overhead, the foghorn sounds two notes, one long, one short, not like the bass boom of the Breaksea lightship, but a high soprano double-note, and again, every fifteen seconds. After the shock we can't stop laughing, and I lie listening to the mournful sound. Occasionally it falls silent, then begins again, automatically, ten minutes after detecting fog.

6   Christine Evans, *Selected Poems* (Seren, 2003).

Morning. The wind strengthens and the fog clears. We meet Christine in the chapel, resplendent in her waterproofs, in the pulpit reading bits of the Bible to Esther, scientific researcher, and Peggy the Labrador. We plan the children's workshops. It'll be too rough for their crossing tomorrow, but the outlook is better for Wednesday. Each class will divide into two groups, and Esther and Ben will take them to examine the seashore, then Christine and I will take a group each to write. One class in the morning, one in the afternoon.

Who, apart from the bones of twenty thousand saints, is on the island? Christine and Ernest's son Colin, fisherman and farmer; Dei the shepherd; his wife Pauline; Dafydd the manager, and his wife. Others are visiting. Richard, engineer, is here to mend the generator. And there's Steve, the bird man. Various visitors are lodging or renting the houses. Arfon Hughes, the Enlli Trust architect, and his wife Betty are at Nant, and Peter Hope-Jones, photographer, is staying at Carreg Fach. Today on the track I met Gwen Newton from Cheshire, who is surveying the island for the lovely wild flower, eyebright. What a mission! She loves poetry, is a fan of R.S. Thomas, and is learning Welsh.

The island is almost treeless, though some of the gardens have a few apple trees and hawthorns. Recently a single specimen of an apple tree unique to the island was discovered, and is now named and propagated as the Bardsey Apple.

Social events on the island: an excellent dinner with Christine and Ernest; a private view of Paul Lewin's island paintings in the lighthouse – we buy one – and a poetry reading with a larger audience than some I've given on shore in so-called civilised places with proper toilets, baths, shops. Just about the whole island turns out. Twenty-five people, maybe?

And next day the children's workshops are lovely, with much good work achieved. The workroom in the lighthouse flowers with their drawings and poems.

The last day: home across the sound, to the car, and a heatwave. From home, more than a hundred miles by road, but much closer across the curve of Cardigan Bay, on a clear day we can see the mountains of Snowdonia and the long line of Llŷn, with the blue humpback of Enlli at the end of the peninsula, and on fine evenings the five flashes of the lighthouse, warning.

Two summers: 2006, and 2007. The hottest, driest summer in Britain for a generation followed by the wettest since records began. The long light of summer, rain or shine, sets me reflecting upon joy – how it survives and revives us in a world that would make us despair. I reflect too on its opposite, the stone in the heart. Not ecstasy and agony. Just ordinary joy, and everyday down-heartedness. The season brings other contrasts to attention too: stillness and movement, sound and silence, company and solitude.

Sometimes you stand still, stunned by the beauty of it all, as if something had been started from its lair right there in your ribcage. You're in love with the planet and with life itself. It is the life-urge. It's what may save the planet, stop the wars, cage the killers, overwhelm ideologues and fanatics if there's enough of it. A flash of joy keeps hope burning, makes being alive worthwhile. It's ordinary, human, private, intimate. Joy is more than wellbeing, a well of being, a being well. It is a physical thrill within the echo-chambers of the heart, the ventricles of blood. It feels entirely sensuous. Joy seems to come from the body. The 'heavy heart' of a dark mood, of worry, or grief, seems to come from the mind, yet we feel that too in our bodies, as a physical burden.

Out of stillness and silence comes a roar of sound. The hot blue sky is ripped by a low flying military jet on an exercise. The shock feels not unlike a thrill of joy, an electric ripple of blood from the body's core that leaves the fingertips tingling, but this time it is unpleasant. It leaves behind disturbance, not wellbeing. It's about knowing what a warplane is, and what it represents. It's a cargo of violence dumped in the mind. An ex-RAF man once told me that our house, a small white landmark on the hill, is used as one of the RAF's 'targets' on mock bombing exercises. I can't clean my mind of that. Haifa, I think. Beirut. Gaza. Iraq. Afghanistan. Lebanon.

Most of us love light. The long light of summer evenings in Britain, as much as their warmth, makes midsummer so lovely, so easy. Like summers in childhood, like the illustrations in A.A. Milne, Peter Rabbit's discovery of the soporific effect of lettuce, images from *Swallows and Amazons*. And the smells of summer. Fields, lanes, main roads, farmyards, and our garden –

once a stackyard, surrounded in June by laburnum in full bloom. Sometimes there's a year when it's more opulent than usual. Does dawdling under its waterfalling yellow, inhaling the scent, count as the deadly sin of sloth? Surely it's right to squander a little time on transient, seasonal things. There are times when missing a chance is a sin against life. We are encircled by it. At such a moment Blaen Cwrt is an island.

Heatwave. Monsoon

July

2006. By the first week in July laburnum and birdsong are over. In June our car pulls a crowd in the car park in Carmarthen, its roof and bonnet gold-leafed with petals which even the 23-mile drive to town has not unstitched. The path and driveway are inlaid gold. Such mosaics I have not seen since a visit to Registan, the palace of Tamburlaine the Great in Samarkand. July, the fallen flowers are brown and shrivelled. and we are left with thousands of seed-pods dangling from the trees and the ground littered with dead petals. The seeds are poisonous. A light has gone out in the garden. Once midsummer day is past, light slips through our fingers, a few minutes a day.

On the thirtieth of June the blackbird sings all day, a soloist in a beech tree with a chorus of hidden willow warblers, wrens, tits, finches and a descant of unidentified others. In the evening the song thrush has sung all spring and early summer from the summit in the ash tree. It likes to sing silhouetted on the topmost twig of the tree, a counter-tenor in the spotlight of the westering sun. How can the voice of a bird thrill the human heart so power-fully? As far as the thrush is concerned it is simply giving utterance to a message, perhaps about territory. Maybe the joy the sound can trigger is because of its associations with the long light evenings of summer. But I think we love it for the music, and the voice with its clear notes, phrases and variations, its two- or three-times repeated refrain. It touches us because it is beautiful.

From the first day of July, birdsong is switched off. Birds fall silent. It happens overnight. Though expected, for a day or two it turns the mood. No call but an occasional distant wood pigeon, sometimes the shrill sob of a stray pheasant, and more often the scream of wheeling swallows. Then silence. For a few days, I am lost, as if unprepared for this annual shift in things. The silence, the shrivelling, the fallen minutes of light. Something is over. For a few days I feel unsettled, deprived of my pleasures. I am used to savouring colour, sound and scent. Then I notice other colours – the faraway blond of hay-fields after baling, the old-Persian-carpet red of the acer right next to the buttery yellow of hypericum; and other sounds – the fields purr with tractors, the high whine and rattle of silage machines. A working countryside comes to life. There are other scents: wild roses in the lane, and the rising heat wakes the honeysuckle, and the bitter, delicious after-smell of azalea which persists long after the flowers have gone.

So the focus shifts. Stillness is replaced by movement, idle pleas-ures by activity. The air spins with swallows. Gethin comes to shear the sheep. To avoid bringing our flock – three rams, twelve ewes and their sixteen lambs – up through the hay to the barn to shear them, we decide to power the electric shears with a gener-ator and to set up half a mile away by the stream at the foot of the fron where the flock is grazing. David loads hurdles and the gener-ator into the pick-up and drives round along the lanes to the gate at the bottom of our land where Fron Blaen Cwrt meets Fron Felen. Fron Blaen Cwrt, the Blaen Cwrt slope, named after the smallholding it's always been part of; Fron Felen, the yellow slope, named after the gorse that turns the whole slope gold in early summer. There are always some flowers on gorse, even in mid-winter. As the saying goes, 'When the gorse is out of blossom, kissing's out of fashion.'

Later, I cross the fields with Siani to help herd the sheep into the pen that David has built from hurdles. To reach the shearing place I keep close to the hedge to avoid crushing the hay in Cae Blaen Cwrt, along the avenue of hornbeams and down through Cae Bach, all shimmering with seeding long grasses and flowers. All the way I wear a hem of butterflies. Siani swims the fields in a cloud of her own, snapping at the air as she dog-paddles the deep grass. Never, never so many butterflies in the fields, most in powdery browns, amber, red-gold, speckled, edged and dotted, and all on the move: Meadow Browns, Gatekeepers, Small Heaths, Ringlets, High Brown Fritillaries. And, by the gate that sings in the wind, a Five Bar Burnet Moth, red, black and cream like the lining of an opera cloak.

Is the profusion of butterflies caused by the hot, dry summer? Or can we attribute the great number of the insects to the fact that our grasses grow without chemicals or fertiliser, without early mowing for silage, or repeat harvesting? Mowing too early gives grasses no chance to flower. My butterfly book, published in 1982, describes the High Brown Fritillary as common and widespread in England and Wales. According to a report in the *Guardian* on 22 July 2006, the High Brown Fritillary, along with up to sixteen other species of butterfly, is in serious decline and already extinct in seven counties of south-east England, due to urban sprawl and industrial farming.

Gethin arrives. He lays down the shearing platform where each sheep will dance on clickety heels until he turns her over, sits her on her rear end, holds and calms her before beginning to work quickly and deftly, sliding the buzzing electric clippers between her skin and her fleece with never a nip or a graze. In minutes she is naked and cool and calling for her lambs. Her fleece lies, the clean white side up and looking much too big for her, ready to be rolled and stored in the woolsack.

A night-shower scarcely lays the dust. Dawn, and the heat rises. The heatwave persists through June and July. We are having a terrace built all along the east and south glass walls of the dining room. Phil the builder arrives at eight every morning. Sounds. The song of the cement-mixer, the gravelly growl of the digger loading stones, the approaching rumble of the Muck-Truck wheeling each load over the grass. These are good sounds. They do not spoil my concentration, writing in my circle of solitude at the garden table under the chestnut tree. As I write, Phil and his assistant, Gareth, move in a steady work rhythm through the day, enjoying the sun, the scents, the red kite over the field as much as I do. The foundations are laid, and now they are building sandstone walls to the north and south of the terrace. The sandstones for the walls are rescued from the fields, long fallen buildings and old walls, supplemented by a lorry-load from the quarry in the village. The north wall will mark the boundary between private and public space, between garden and the drive, path and front door. The curved south wall marks the boundary between our work and nature's. Nature will, I hope, grow lichens on the wall, spill ferns over it, and scatter it with beech leaves in autumn, soon blurring the border between the tame and the wild. The terrace is an L-shaped outdoor room, an extension of the indoors, a pavement between us and the fields.

In July the sound of our neighbours takes over from the birds of early summer, up and down the lane with tractors, tedding hay in the fields. A light aircraft dawdles in the sky with no destination in mind, like a child on a bike in the street. From early childhood I remember a slow light plane in a blue sky as one of summer's sounds. It turns silver in the sun as the kites turn copper.

Turn. There is alchemy in the word as well as choreography.

Evening. Eight swallows – they are multiplying – and three kites on the wing. The big barley field below Cae Blaen Cwrt has been cut, and there'll be carnage for kites in the lying barley. How do they know? The swallows are more daring this year. The young ones sometimes wheel through the house. They arrow in through the porch, where they perch a moment on the wall light, screaming, then through the kitchen, the garden room and out of the wide open French windows. Then again, and again, like kids on skateboards. When this skateboarding phase is over they return to their hunting-grounds over the field. I count at least twelve birds in the air, the latest, newly fledged brood being fed on the wing by their parents and older siblings.

(Months later, replacing the lightbulb in the porch, we discover the incomplete mud-cup of a swallow's nest. That explains the wheeling through the porch and house, and those brief moments of pause as they perched on the wall light. They were house hunting.)

A family of long-tailed tits whispers in the willow copse at the end of the garden when we go for a walk to look at the sunset. 'I love them. They are so discreet,' David says. And so they are, murmuring their novenas in their cloisters and clerestories.

Dust. Sand. I know dust can be made of anything, and that house dust is mainly composed of our own skin. I know that any stone can become sand. But what is sandstone?

I come indoors to escape the dust that flies from the blade of the stone-saw. The men cut sandstone slabs to size. I keep an eye on the activity through glass walls, aware that glass too is made of sand, silica, lead, or some such recipe. I ponder the wondrous alchemy that turns the opacity of rock, metal and other stuff into transparency. Earth, dust, sand and sandstone are all being worked here, and they are all one, the stuff of the earth itself. Their colours are in harmony. The bone-dry, stony, red-ochre earth has been ironed flat with the wonderfully named whacker-plate which dashes away like a smoothing iron, removing the creases from this scrap of Ceredigion, a Bendigeidfran stamping stones and earth to dust. Buckets of water, shovels of sand, cement and lime are turned into a grey, doughy mortar and barrowed to the terrace. Mortar is dolloped onto the smoothed earth, and sandstone slabs, four different sizes, laid down in a careful and pleasing pattern. The men eye the spirit level, tap the corners of stones with a hammer, add a little mortar here, trowel away a little there. The stone-saw whines as it cuts the slabs to size for the edge. Stone dust veils the sunlight. The earth-dust is ochre. The sand from the quarry a mile away is grey-gold. Stones picked from the land left over from old walls and buildings long fallen rise again to build the low terrace walls. They are grey with a touch of rust like the stones brought from the quarry when our own stone runs out. The freshly cut stones are sharp edged, and will need time to mellow and match the recycled stones. Grey sandstone tinged with red-ochre. I turn to my trusty *Guide to Minerals, Rocks and Fossils*, a favourite reference book.

Sandstone. Texture: medium-grained, grains all about the same size, subangular to rounded. Structure: bedding apparent, ripple marks common. Concretions and fossils may be found. Mineralology: Quartz is the main component, often with feldspar, mica or other minerals. The grains may be cemented by silica, calcite or iron oxides.

Sedimentary rock, laid down and rippled by the seas millions of years ago, now quarried and cut and laid down for us to walk on. When the men have gone home we walk on the lovely space of the terrace, the new-ancient sandstone slabs steady and level underfoot. Sunlight and cats love it. The cats choose sun-warmed stones, or the shade of an acer in a pot. The dog flops down and stretches with a little groan of pleasure. The old longhouse with its newish glass room stands its ground as if it had always expected to be rescued from the sea of grass. It settles, weighted on the earth, as easy on the sandstone terrace as a church on its piazza.

I look down. Ripples formed by seas that flowed here, in this very place, pre-Ceredigion, millions of years ago in the long, slow making of the planet. The sight and the texture of the ripples in the warm stones under my bare feet make me dizzy. Just thinking about the shove of tides over the settling sediments make me dizzy. I touch a ripple with my toe. I feel the ancient Iapetus Ocean shift in it. I am walking on water.

Thunderstorms. Distant drums and the rooms electric. We count tigers to estimate how far away the storm is – too far for a drench of rain. We don't get many thunderstorms here in the west. The mighty throat of the river Severn seems to suck electricity from the western approaches of the Atlantic and the Celtic sea, and funnel most thunderstorms up-river along the border of Wales and England into the heartland. Most such storms miss us by miles in Ceredigion, and bypass Cardiff too, resulting, they say, in a malady known as the Cardiff headache. I remember the Cardiff headache, but I also remember once watching lightning for hours from the bay window of our upstairs flat in a suburb high on a hill looking over the city. The lightning seemed to hang in the sky over the docks and the Bristol Channel like strings of Christmas tinsel. A marvel, a terror, a glory. Like the storms in Limousin, where lightning over the distant mountains of the Dordogne seemed too far away to be frightening, but wonderful enough to sit watching late in a balmy night garden.

The first day of August. 2006. The heatwave breaks. A lovely, long, stone-washing shower of rain on the terrace. Dust flows from the stones onto the grass. Leaves sip drops from the sky. I'm enjoying *The Secret Life of Trees* by Colin Tudge. I consult it to find out how much a tree drinks. Big trees drink 500 litres a day, sucking it from the earth by osmosis and transpiring it into the air to fall somewhere else as rain. Californian redwoods get most of their water from mists from the Pacific. I suppose our trees share breath with the Atlantic when they can. Chestnut trees in London are in trouble from the drought. One of our beech trees is shedding leaves already.

Our biggest hayfield, Cae Delyn – the harp field – slopes to the south. It lies in the heat of the sun all day. One year it yields 150 bales of sweet hay. The year of the drought the grass grows too little to bother mowing. A beautiful field, full of wild flowers and butterflies, it lacks shade, and it's thirsty. How much does a field drink? How lovely it is to rejoice at a fall of rain! We can't live without it. During the long, cold, dry months of winter and spring I wrote a sequence about water, and rain. Did it count as a rain-spell?

No rain since the shower. Poetry makes nothing happen.

The third brood of four young swallows has flown. One watches from a ledge in the barn while the plumber attends to the new water tank. David and the plumber lift a board from the platform on which the big tank rests. Under it, two toads. We are never alone. A poet-friend and I once found a toad when moving a huge pile of stones. I said: 'What has the toad been eating down there all that time?' He said: 'What has it been thinking about?'

2007. Another summer. The wettest ever recorded. We can no longer take the seasons for granted. No April showers this year, just weeks of drought and a 30 degree Celsius heatwave instead. No flaming June. No season of mists. No winter snow. The spring heatwave over, rain begins to fall. The Jetstream, a ribbon of air lying longitudinally over the Atlantic, is stalled too far south, sucking precipitation off the ocean, driving it in successive depressions over our islands. So it rains torrentially throughout June and July. Floodwater overwhelms Yorkshire, Oxfordshire, Hereford, Gloucester. People wade in village streets, animals are marooned on islands of grazing over broken rivers, cornfields are destroyed, hay lies rank in the fields. Our terrace washes and washes itself in the downpour, stones cleaning themselves like the man on the highway embankment in Mumbai, washing the heat and dust of the city from his hair, his limbs, his body in a gift of cold, clean silver streaming from a tap. It is strange warm rain, tropical rain. Our glass doors are left open to the sound of it, as in a tropical country where glass doors are kept wide open in the heat, shaded by deep verandahs beyond which torrential rain falls. Our moat dances. The stones leap with steel-tipped dancing shoes. Our new gutters gush into the moat, which overflows, as it is designed to do, into the stream, for once an important water-course carrying its load to the rivers and the sea. There is much entertainment to be had from watching such rain.

There are more slugs and they are larger than I have ever seen before. They are eating everything in the garden. They even climb the poles to eat the runner beans.

The Jetstream shifts, the rain stops, but summer doesn't settle. It can't quite recover from the idea of cloud from the sea and an imminence of rain. The leeks are heraldic, the sort Owain Glyndŵr's army might have worn to battle, 'Climbing Snowdon / With their woad on.' The beans have climbed out of trouble. They like rain. After all that warm moist air, the cucumbers and tomatoes proliferate in the polytunnel. The sweetcorn is surprisingly good. As July ends, in one fine hot week between showers we get in the hay that we thought we had lost, we and our neighbours in the field loading 125 bales. The particularly heavy crop of grass after all the rain has yielded a scented, pale green hay that sings in your hand as you test its dryness. I learned that trick of 'listening' to the hay when the old man from Allt Maen was alive. I watched him twenty years ago, walking his field, lifting a few strands to his ear, listening to its whispers.

Getting the hay in after the long deluge feels so good. It feels as if something is forgiven.

Kite, Buzzard, Crow

August

A flashback to kites falling on flesh. They appear out of the blue, at first just one or two specks in the sky, then more, until they are soaring in from all points over the mountains. Two or three hundred red kites firing in the sun as they flex and turn, homing down to a farm near Rhayader in mid-Wales. There, in a small field, fresh, raw meat is tipped from a trailer at the same hour every day. Diversification in agriculture has rarely been so imaginatively conceived. This is theatre.

Once the news is out, every kite in the mountain heartland of Wales knows it. The day in spring when I visit, a BBC camera team is preparing to film. Iolo Williams, 'the bird man', here to present the programme, tells me it is very likely that our kites from seventy miles away in Ceredigion are among these visitors, and that kites come to the feeding site from as far away as Yorkshire. How do they know? Do they have mobile phones?

First come the crows, minesweepers clearing the ground for the great arrival. Then the buzzards, outriders taking the risk to get a first snatch at the feast. Once the crows and buzzards have retreated to the trees with their share of flesh, and the lie of the land looks safe, the first kite appears, distantly floating on the thermals above the mountains. According to the farm's website, on rare occasions, during strange weather maybe, the crows and the buzzards have failed to arrive to feed. On those days the kites eye the ground from afar but come no closer. But today all is well. Crow and buzzard descend and fly off, then singly, in twos, tens, hundreds, the angelic host blazes down on a field of blood.

Now it is August, and here, over our fields, seventy miles south-west of that spectacular daily event, kites are a common sight these days. This scavenger of the streets of medieval London was perse-cuted, shot by gamekeepers, its nests plundered by egg collectors until it was Britain's rarest bird. A few birds survived in its heart-land in the mountains of mid-Wales, though at worst, according to reports of studies using DNA evidence, its numbers were reduced to the offspring of a single female.

The other day a huge combine harvester was at work in our neighbour's big barley field. All day, as the monstrous machine growled up and down the field, four kites haunted the sky, causing consternation to the buzzards and a crowd of crows competing to feed on fresh kill: crushed mice, voles, rabbits, frogs.

A kite is a parable of beauty and violence. Its obsession, its golden eye burning the ground for blood, the unflinching instinct to survive. Riding the thermals, it flexes its wings and long forked tail in independent movements – the only bird which can do that – flaunting its auburns, manoeuvring the wind. As it drops on injured prey or carrion it scarcely touches the ground. Such lazy grace, such beauty, such savagery!

A ewe died deep in the gorse last winter, too far inside the thicket to be discovered except by foxes and crows. Gorse makes a fortified city, arched, aisled and alley-wayed for fox and badger or an old sheep seeking respite from wind and rain. The kite circled, waiting, while the crows and the buzzards ripped open the carcase. Then it descended in slow, elegant circles, fell on the body, and gorged. Flamboyance – that's the word I want, flame on air – its reds all the more fiery against the clean bow of white under the span of its wings, the black bars on its tail. Beautiful, gorging, gorgeous.

Twice, in a few days, on the wet morning grass, David has found a mangled animal, the size of a stoat or squirrel, its head opened by something like a hooked beak, its fur drenched and colourless. Over the field a kite carries a stoat in its claw, the stoat which, as

R.S. Thomas wrote, 'sips at the brimmed rabbit'.[1] With one word, 'sips', the poet turns the rabbit into a vessel of blood. So, in turn, the kite sips the stoat. A holy communion.

Our hay is a swaying sea of grasses and wild flowers, yet to be mowed, tedded, raked, baled, carried and stored. The weather is hot and still. I can see for miles. Not a hundred miles, as sometimes, one day last week, for example, though more often in winter. Richard Fortey's *The Earth: An Intimate History* begins, 'It should be difficult to lose a mountain but it happens all the time.' 'Vesuvius', he writes, 'slips in and out of view.'[2] Across Cardigan Bay to the north-west, Snowdonia, and the long finger of the Llŷn peninsula, lie lost in sea-haze for most of the summer. The first cold morning of autumn, and it'll be there, lying on the sea like a legend.

I wade the hay. It smells of so many sweet nectars and bitter liquors that I'm dizzy inhaling it and only bees could untangle one scent from another. Almonds, mint, dark chocolate, mysterious herbal infusions and tisanes. I stand listening. The grass sings with insects and airs, the very field from which I heard the wood-voices when I wrote 'Letter from a Far Country' in the 1970s. There is no birdsong in the woods today. Except for the crows, and the lament of a pair of collared doves, August is silent. The birds have nothing to say, not warning, love song, lullaby or territorial cry.

The forecast is good, a week of warm, dry weather promised. Gethin is coming to mow the hay tonight. The seeding grasses and flowers include yellow rattle and tormentil. The inspector from Tir Gofal[3] is pleased, as these plants are signifiers of unfertilised, chemical-free land. Their presence proves that our land is returning to a natural state and we've earned our 'Tir Gofal' status. Some of our fields have never been ploughed or 'improved'. 'Unimproved land' is the great accolade in Tir-Gofal-speak. We

1 'Aim', *Experimenting with an Amen* (Macmillan, 1986).
2 HarperCollins, 2004.
3 Literally, 'Land Care'. The government scheme that grant-aids land managed for biodiversity.

glow like praised children. The flower and grass names are a litany, their names as heady as their smells. Next door the fertilised, weed-killed fields are a bright, unbroken green, free of flower, molehill or worm.

When most of our neighbours were haymaking it was too soon for us. Having signed up our land for what's best for biodiversity, we are not permitted to mow before 14 July. Then we must wait for the weather and our neighbours to be free to help. I'm always anxious and obsessed by weather forecasts until the hay is safe home.

The hay is cut. Killed. In Welsh we 'kill the hay', *lladd y gwair*. It's an apt word for it. 'Kill' brings images: a field mouse, a kite, an old suicide, and a more recent one. The old suicide was Marged's who died in the 1930s. Her story is history and I reflect upon it with outrage rather than sorrow. She died in her fifties for the lack of a welfare state. When her grandfather Benni and her aunt Nani died, their pensions died with them. Marged inherited the house: a long-house, its two rooms, croglofft and small barn under one long roof. At one end was the tiny dairy, at the other the lean-to beudy where she milked her cow. She had one field, her garden, the spring where she drew water in a bucket. She had a pigsty, and a pig, and prob-ably hens. She had no income. As a house-owner she could not draw on parish funds. She depended for her survival on cultivating her scrap of land and on her good neighbours' generosity. That dark winter day, ill with flu, she hanged herself. David's uncle recalls people who still remembered hearing the cow lowing to be milked.

The other suicide is a fresh hurt. Our best hayfield, Cae Delyn, named for its harp shape, lies aslant a south-facing slope. Its cut and raked hay-rows viewed from the high road above the valley are like harp-strings. Cae Delyn looks down to where the Glowan flows through lush grazing, and across the valley to where fields rise about two farms and their buildings. The closer farm is hidden in trees. The other farm and its buildings lie in open land. From that more distant farm, when the wind's in the right direction, we might hear someone revving a tractor, or driving a fencepost with a sledgehammer. There, a few years ago, a young man we had known killed himself. His father found him one early morning in the cow shed. The tragedy lies like heat haze over the valley.

The new-mown hay smells of vanilla, cinnamon, camomile. I love the smell, the curve of the hill contour-lined with hay-rows, the prospect of big machines and the purposeful busyness of tedding, tossing the hay to dry in the sun, raking, baling, the swaying load making its way home.

The tedding machine behind the tractor is a contraption with two airy wheels like the Big Wheels at the fair. Each big wheel bears a circle of spidery spinners – like the chairs on the Big Wheel. Twice a day the tedder tosses the hay in the warm air for the last breath of damp to expire. In a few days it'll be raked into rows again and baled into old-fashioned Weetabix shapes, each small enough for one person to lift.

It's real hay, the kind you must store in a barn, the only sort you can feed to horses. Gethin says it's good to smell old-fashioned hay again. Yes, it's good and sweet, but you need five days of dry weather to cut and gather it in. Most of our neighbours now use the quicker, more secure big bale system which they call 'haylage'. It is hay, not silage. I don't blame them. It's the only sure way in a poor summer. But the huge plastic-wrapped bales left piled in the fields are an eyesore – even the name is ugly – and they leave the old stone barns of the countryside empty of purpose. So the barns fall stone by stone back to the earth, or are sold for house conversion. So the landscape changes.

It is a good feeling, to be hot and exhausted, knowing the hay is in, relishing the neighbourliness of the work, knowing the hay will sweeten the barn all winter.

One year of unsettled summer weather we despaired of ever getting in the hay. Then came a sudden dry spell, and every farm, field and lane hummed with mowers and balers. We thought there'd be no time or weather left for us. One day our neighbour arrived to mow. Next day a huge tractor towing a baler turned up unannounced, driven by a friendly stranger who roared in through the gate with a wave and in a trice had big-baled our hay. Someone had remembered us when their fields were done, and had sent him along. Then a neighbour brought us small bales to swap for the big ones, knowing we haven't the equipment to lift them. At times like this I think the whole valley is one farm, and its people a commune of workers. No one seems to organise such an event. It just happens. A dry day, and we drop everything else. We're on the phone to cancel, postpone, make our excuses. Being self-employed makes it possible. Then everyone is in the field, working, each at his or her own pace, performing a light or heavy task.

My senses are busy with all this while my mind hurts with the private argument and the big troubled world. There is always a war somewhere. Was it always so? And nature, with flood, hurricane and earthquake, would shake us off the planet.

I argue in my head with a novelist who says he hates poetry because it is 'complicated and abstract'. My novelist friend is well-known and highly respected. Complicated? Abstract? Yes, bad poetry is like that. Good poetry is layered with secrets, observant, true, the best so simple it can stop your heart. Shakespeare. Donne. Hopkins. Yeats. Emily Dickinson. R.S. Thomas. Hughes. And many living poets too, young and old.

It's my fault. I accidentally provoke the argument by saying that most poets read novels but many novelists don't read any poetry at all. Five of us in the bar between events at a literary conference, the novelist, three passionate poetry fans, and one who likes to listen to poetry but also loves the silent pleasure of reading a novel for the 'world' it offers. The three poetry-lovers also understand the reader's total immersion in the new world of a novel, the page-turning power of the story. All five of us confess that we rarely read a novel more than once, but the poetry-lovers all read favourite poems over and over, searching for the secret of their power, finding something new at every reading, yet never fathoming the mystery.

Reading a novel and reading a poem are completely different ways of reading. There is no comparison. One drives you on, page after page. The other stops you dead, stops your breath as if you saw the burning bush. One is a journey, the other is a spell.

Between novels, I'm re-reading Richard Fortey's *The Earth*, Annie Dillard's *An American Childhood*, and I've rediscovered David Constantine's *Collected Poems*. A novel is a journey without

stations. Maybe that's why novels are good to read on the train, or
on those rare but unendurable sleepless journeys through the night
when time is slow and the scenery dark and troubled. When the
novel is finished I close the book, and if it's any good it unfolds in
my mind for hours, days, weeks, forever if it is a truly great novel,
by Tolstoy, Dickens, George Eliot. *The Earth* I read slowly,
pausing to re-read a passage, to be amazed, to insert bookmarks to
find my way back to certain pages. I learn a new fact, new words.
The excitement of discovery and a new technical lexicon are good
for a poet. I take up the notebook, scribble a phrase, an image. The
poetry of ideas, physics, stones, natural history, facts simply and
beautifully explained by an eloquent enthusiast schooled in a disci-
pline new to me will always start a poem from its form.

   So to poetry. For days I couldn't pass the first two of David
Constantine's poems that I read, on the last page in the book. Do
other people read collections of poetry backwards? Should I
arrange my next collection to allow for this? One of the poems is
'A Trilobite in the Wenlock Shales'. I am stunned. It is the perfect
example of what I'd like to offer all poetry sceptics. Look! I'd say.
Listen! It's a spell, a magic trick, a key to your heart made by a man
who doesn't even know you. This is the thousandth time it's
happened to me. One friend says the first poem that did it for her
was Seamus Heaney's 'Death of a Naturalist'. Another cites Ted
Hughes's 'Thrushes'. Simon Armitage quotes Hughes too. This is
reading of quite a different order. It is physical. Such a poem will
lie in the strata of my mind, whole, to be woken again like the
long-extinct trilobite in the stone.

I'm watering tomatoes and French beans in the polytunnel. A hot
job. I consider the carnivorous ways of nature. The female black-
bird is with me, silent, scuttling close to me under the leafy arcades
of French beans. Jac dozes, one eye open, on his favourite pile of
old hay. It looks dangerous for the blackbird, so I reach into the
beans to shoo her away, actually nudging her feathers. She scuttles
off, trotting busily across the earth. The swallows wheel over the
barn, diving in through the gap above the big doors with their
beaks full of insects, then out and over the garden and fields, two

adults and eight young from the first two broods, all feeding the last brood, nestlings which must get strong and learn to fly with only weeks to prepare for the flight to Africa. It's beautiful and incredible to watch this – a whole family of wild creatures engaged in such unselfish cooperation. It shows how evolution can favour altruism.

Flashback to August 2005, and a week teaching in Oxford. I am tutoring at Christ Church for Tower Poetry. My students are a group of young people chosen for their exceptional talent as poets. Most are good but several students stand out. What I find exciting is when, after what I hope is an inspirational half hour setting up the idea, the young writers fall silent and begin to write, filling an empty page. In an hour those pages are full, and we read to each other, and most of the poems, though rough and raw, are alive with energy.

When teaching is finished I relish walking in Christ Church gardens as if I own the place. I love the foot-worn stone stairs, the hand-worn balustrades, the cold stone corridors, cloisters and arcades, the carefully memorised track to my room, along paths, round corners, up and down steps and stairs and through doorways into secret gardens like roofless rooms. My room overlooks Christ Church meadows. I enjoy its balcony and stone-mullioned windows, the sash windows built inside them, surely fifteen feet high, the summer hum and grassy breath of lawnmowers, poplars brightening with a sudden shiver like a turning shoal of mackerel. I walk out into the city, sit in cafés writing, watching and listening. One evening in a restaurant I hear a group of young women talk about class, and how distanced they feel from their families now they are at university. What a burden the English sense of class must be! Never once did I feel distanced from my late coal miner father-in-law, Glyndŵr Thomas, who loved poetry, photography, art and opera, or my mother-in-law, still at ninety enjoying music and good books. When, years ago, I phoned Glyndŵr to tell him I was going to the Soviet Union on a writers' exchange visit, and that I would be visiting Samarkand, he broke into verse:

> For lust of knowing what shall not be known
> You take the golden road to Samarkand.

He had learned Flecker's poem by heart long ago, and kept it there. That is how poetry works. Like the trilobite, it lies quietly in the mind to be reawoken.

While I walked and taught and wrote and slept, astronauts in the good ship *Discovery* sailed safe home to earth in a desert in California, and a trapped submarine was freed and rose to the surface of a Russian sea. Who do we think we are? Travellers afloat inside bubbles of air in deep space, and in the deepest oceans. Not satisfied with the generous air of terra firma where we belong, we long for that vertiginous place beyond the edge of world and mind, where the poetry is.

Home, to find this year's hay is in: 167 bales, twenty-five for us, and the rest stowed at Mynachlog. We don't need more to feed our little flock over winter. We still have some left from last year. When the cats come in from the night they will smell of the hay they think is their own.

2006. The end of August, before the children go back to school, a lovely family visit. On the last evening we decide to walk on the cliffs before driving to Aberaeron for dinner. We take the cliff-path from Cwmtydu to Castell Bach, the semi-circular Iron Age fort on the cliff's edge. Below, above the tideline on the little beach, lies a seal pup, pure white and only days old. The children have been longing to see a seal and they scramble down the path, banned from too close an approach. The pup lies still as a white stone among the pebbles, as they always do, but my binoculars show its black eyes bloody. Abandoned. The gulls – those kites of the sea – have begun their plunder.

All summer, war and murder, yet a dead seal pup can still hurt. Like the young swallow Jac snatched in the barn as David opened the big doors to let it escape. Slaughter out there in the world is huge, the numbers too great to imagine. I held the swallow. It was warm, perfect. These are metaphors for the greater slaughter, for the mess we make of things. Is that why the weightless warmth of a swallow in the hand or the sight of a dead seal pup still hurts?

We hasten back along the cliff, driven by the sight of a vast black shower dragging its skirts over the sea from Ireland. Soon we are stung by hailstones and soaked to the skin. We have to rush home for hot showers, towelled hair and dry clothes before going for dinner, which is the more delicious for the soaking.

The family gone, I look back on summer. Birds. Books. Bees. A field of hay. The August silence of birds. The tame female blackbird. The family of swallows. Buzzards. Kites. A crowd of crows that swirl apparently without purpose, sometimes resting on five invisible wires in the middle distance, annotating the air with a tune you could sing. Everyone says they've never seen so many crows. The bees are wild and tame: bumblebees, and honey bees stashing gold in the combs of their many-storeyed hive under the apple trees at the end of the vegetable garden.

A friend visits. Charles Bennett. We talk about reading poetry – I'm still fretting! – and the different ways we read different types of text. He says, 'We don't read a poem. We scan it. We say "This fits here, and this fits there",' and as he explains his hands act it out, touching the imaginary poem on the table. This reminds me that Helen Vendler said, 'a line of poetry is a glance'. Yet the poem is also a heard melody, a song held true by cadence and word-order, 'the right words in the right order'.

Later, I think of a poem as, in a way, like a painting. After the first reading certain words or phrases become luminous, and the shaping imagery of the poem separates and reshapes in the mind. Instead of knowing its place, the luminous word shifts, restless, affecting not just the line where it is placed, but the whole poem, like an ice-cube in a glass of water. Like a little red figure in a classical landscape. Like a kite over a hayfield.

The Brown Hairstreak Butterfly

September

Right on cue the first chestnut leaves fall. Always the first tree to undress for autumn. Spider's webs weighted with beads. Crane-flies. Blackberries. Plums.

Every morning there are fallen plums on the grass, and if we're lucky we get them before the slugs do. They are small and red-purple, sweet enough to reach up and take straight from the tree to eat as we pass through the garden. Two of the three trees lean towards the ground, acute angles of wizened old prunus wood, their foliage thin scribbles against the sky. The third is a bit more of a tree, more upright and spreading. Our washing lines are strung between them, which useful purpose no doubt saved them from the axe until we learned their true worth, surprised by their benef-icence the first year we were here. No one has been able to identify the trees, so we get Tir Gofal points for preserving them. No one else round here seems to have one. Perhaps we are nurturing the Blaen Cwrt plum, rare, maybe, as the Bardsey Apple discovered growing on Enlli and nowhere else. Cuttings were taken, and its offspring now flourish in a commercial orchard.

Minutes of light slip from the days. How I miss the company of birds! Only the swallows still swoop over the garden. I dread their departure. The blackbird is now only seen dashing between trees, and his mate no longer forages the ground. A robin is singing. Winter will bring the birds home.

David has just walked in with a *siani blewog* on his finger. A woolly caterpillar! It's not the first – I have taken out three or four in the past week. Last night there was a frog in the hall. We have to watch our step. We can't call our home our own these days.

We can't keep up with the vegetable garden. Courgettes, cucumbers, beans, cabbage, beetroot, still some lettuce and rocket. One year the glory was the immortal Cavolo Nero, the pull-and-pick-again Italian kale we planted in the tunnel in summer, forgot during the winter, then discovered flourishing there in the spring. It survived for two years, then, when it grew into a great forest that threatened to engulf the whole tunnel, we pulled it up, and forgot to plant it again.

David lifts the roof off the hive to check the bees – rising aromas of wax and honey, bees crawling through the little trapdoor into the roof-space of their many-storeyed house. The combs are full to the brim. They are busy down at the front door too, worker bees pushing all the drones out to die. Over winter it will be a female household. At dusk if you put your ear to the hive you can hear a million wings keeping the temperature just right. This was a fierce colony when it first arrived a few years ago. Now the bees are calm, and I don't feel nervous about approaching the hive or working in the garden close to them. These are signs of a good queen and an ordered and benign royal household. In summer, if a bee wanders into the house, I put out my finger for it to crawl on, and I take it outside. Bees don't want to sting us. They want to live, so release their stings in extremis only.

2005. David accidentally mows the top off a nest of bumblebees, setting a cloud of the insects into the air. They'd nested in a burrow hidden between the hedge bank, an acer and an old rose where we rarely manage to mow. The terrible blades of the ride-on mower make a hurricane of steel and air. In a moment all they had built has gone, their citadel roofless, a ruined city, with a pathetic cluster of cells revealed, primitive and vulnerable – not at all like the grand wax palaces of honey bees, whose well-stocked larder must keep them alive through the winter. After a moment of consternation, the bumblebees set about the work of repair. In half an hour they have built a dome of moss over the earth burrow. A bee mosque. I think of the hornets' nest in France, and the man with a ladder who came to cut it from the farmhouse eaves, a necessary massacre because our host was dangerously allergic to a hornet sting. And there, in a bucket, lay the smashed remains of a civilisation. The hornets had flown, but the little hornet grubs lay swaddled like babies doomed to die in the ruins of their nursery.

Another parable. A ruined city: the crushing of the bumble bees' nest will always be associated in my mind with New Orleans laid waste by hurricane. We are silenced. Words are too big for themselves. Only the poetry of blues can speak for it.

How to lament and at the same time love nature? There is an edge to it: love is the greater because of loss, life more precious because of death. The red kite, untroubled by such human philosophising, innocent of its own beauty, knows only hunger. It feels its weight on the thermals and it burns, its yellow eye alert for the least thing stirring in the field below.

I could envy the kite's concentration, unselfconscious and undistractable.

September 2007. After the wettest summer ever recorded, the relief of seeing the hay piled in the barn is still with us. It is not that we need much hay for our small flock, but that a field left lying rank with old grass is spoilt for next year too. In spring, its roots choke and too much nitrogen seeps into the soil. It is essential for biodiversity that we mow and clear the field of all gleanings. If left there would be fewer flowers next year, fewer butterflies, beetles, creatures who live in the grass. We let our old rams into Cae Bach, the avenue and Cae Blaen Cwrt to graze them off. One evening Gethin brings nine of Mynachlog's heifers to graze the thick, tufty, unmowable grass on the slopes of Fron Felen. One white, two black and six red heifers, bright-eyed, pink-nosed, curious and frisky and always pleased to see us.

Bill Summerfield, our new Tir Gofal advisor, is aptly named for a man with his job. Is it serendipity? Or does one's name influence one's choice of career? He has come at our invitation to follow up a letter he wrote us earlier this month.

Out of the blue, on the sort of day when the world out there is ugly and violent, work frustrates and persons from Porlock and the Planning Department trouble us by phone and email, a letter arrives from Bill. He writes to ask if we would like to take part in the Brown Hairstreak butterfly conservation project, now in its third year. At the head of the letter is a picture of the butterfly, a beautiful creature with dark brown wings splashed with orange, the under-wings amber and hair-streaked with white. The butterfly has been recorded on land close to ours, and he thinks that our land too might be perfect for it. All we have to do is make sure the conditions are right. This is just the sort of vision we need right now. It says, slow down, focus, consider one small detail in the great complexity that is the world. It reminds us why we live here.

We study the needs of the Brown Hairstreak butterfly. It's a shy creature, rarely seen, and its needs are few but complex, as is the diversity we're nurturing here by intention and neglect. The insect feeds on the young foliage of blackthorn, so if we continue failing to get around to cutting the blackthorn in the hedges, or to cutting only a bit one year, another bit the next, our hedges will continue be perfect for it to lay its eggs. It lives high in mature trees, especially ash, where the butterflies gather to mate and to feed on the honeydew of aphids that are dependent on ash trees and the like. If we fail to fell our big ash trees life will be perfect for our guest. Indeed, perhaps she is here already, hiding high in the canopy, feeding on honeydew.

Friends hear the story. Noting our pleasure at being part of the Brown Hairstreak rescue project, they ask, 'Oh! Have you seen it?' 'No,' we say. 'We may never see it.' They raise eyebrows, but we tell them that just the thought of it is heartening. Just letting it be seems a good thing to do. It is a metaphor, an idea, named but largely invisible, like God.

Bill Summerfield is pleased by the presence of the heifers too. They graze off the long, bleached stalks and old yellowed grass, whereas sheep only nibble short, fresh grasses close to the ground. Sheep bad, cattle good. Cattle also benefit the grass by treading holes in the sward which aerate it and leave bare patches for chancers to germinate, parasol seeds, seed-rich bird droppings, travellers on the wind. Bill looks at the grass above the gorse bank on steep Fron Felen, and the level stretch above the oak wood, and he frowns. 'Partly improved,' he says, disappointed at the sight. 'We don't know how it got that way,' we say. In Tir Gofal terms, unimproved is good, semi-improved is disappointing, improved is bad.

A fine, new tipper trailer has arrived. It is red, with forest-green parts and yellow wheel hubs. It's clean as a toy fresh out of its box, and smells like a just unwrapped Christmas present. David has not stopped grinning since it was delivered. He loads it with leather gloves, pruning shears and chain saw, links it to the tractor and sets off over the land to cut the long gorse hedges above and between Fron Blaen Cwrt and Fron Felen. He is happy as R.S. Thomas's Cynddylan. 'Ah, you should see Cynddylan on his tractor... He's a new man now',[1] I tease, pretending it's no more than a boy's toy, but in truth I too feel the excitement of the trailer's brand new Christmas morning look.

It is the season for cutting and burning the gorse. We could not begin the work until the trailer arrived to carry the huge, heavy, prickly branches to a suitable burning place. We are permitted to burn only on improved or semi-improved land. If we want to burn gorse cuttings on the spot, we must lay down corrugated iron sheets before lighting the fire, and all potash must be removed afterwards. This is because we must not add fertiliser to Tir Gofal land.

One September we cut the overgrown hedge of gorse between our field, Cae Delyn, and Pant Swllt's land, and laid it in a row below the bank, intending to return and burn it within the permitted period for fires, well before the nesting season. Time passed. We were busy with our proper work, the sort that earns a living. The weather was bad. Spring came and we were left with a dilemma. The gorse could not remain on our best hayfield. One April evening, we decided to remove and burn it, examining each

---

1 'Cynddylan on a Tractor', *Welsh Airs* (Poetry Wales Press, 1987).

branch carefully for nests before burning. Darkness fell, and there was just one small pile left for the morning, when David returned to place the last antlers of gorse on the white circle of still-smouldering ashes. The very last branch contained a thrushes' nest holding one very cold blue egg. The nest had been built horizontally parallel to the earth, proving it had been done this season, after the hedge was cut. The thrush must have deserted it the previous evening, alarmed by our presence and the smoke. Burning gorse so late, even long-cut gorse, is a kind of crime. We ought to have cleared it in winter, well before the nesting season.

Gorse has grown so long and so widely in Britain that it has many names. *Ulex galli*, and *Ulex europaeus*, furze, prickly broom, whin, ruffet, frey, goss, and, in Welsh, *eithin*. According to the reference books, there are three kinds of gorse on our land, though I didn't know that until I looked closer. At a glance it's hard to distinguish one from the other. *Ulex europaeus*, European gorse, flowers from December to April, opening to glorious full bloom in spring. Dwarf Furze begins to flower in late spring, and is in full bloom in August. *Ulex galli*, the native Welsh/British gorse, follows, flowering from August to Christmas. So there's never a season without a gorse flower. Late April and May are best here, when the gorse that gives our steep bank, Fron Felen, its name, the yellow slope, turns the whole hill gold, and warmth wakes the coconut scent of it. In May we walk the track inhaling it until we reach the wood where the coconut air is doused by the breath of a hectare of bluebells.

Living gorse contains a highly volatile oil. One match, a twist of newspaper, and the freshly cut gorse catches and the fire roars into life. All we need do is feed it. The gorse fire is greedy and ferocious, and we daren't pause a minute in our cutting and carrying. David chainsaws the branches and I drag them away. We prune away cross-branches and awkward elbows, and lay them on the fire in one direction, using the heaviest to weigh down the others. The green, live branches of gorse burn and die back to an ash so hot that the next armful of cuttings bursts instantly into flame, and next day there will be nothing left but the still hot circle of white ash.

It is cold, the valley below is in deep shadow, and the sun's almost gone from the hill. We're hot and tired from our work and the fire, especially David who aches from hours wielding the chainsaw. There's pleasure in the heat and cold of it, in the contrasts that make each thing vivid: hard outdoor work against the prospect of the ease indoors. In the fading light we pack up, stow the tools in the bright new trailer, thinking of hot baths, a meal, a glass of wine, a book.

There is always a compromise to be made between conserving and using the earth. Fire produces carbon, but if gorse is left to grow unchecked, it will die. Cut gorse can't be left to decay on the fields. We hired a wood shredder once, but it was a slow, noisy and fuel-greedy machine. So we must burn the gorse. At least fire is natural.

Our council's introduction of a good recycling system has changed our old habits from binning rubbish to recycling almost every-thing. Since this began we think about every item, and have developed an easy routine. Ceredigion was slow to introduce recy-cling, but when they did they gave us an excellent system. Basically they take all paper, all plastic, and metal, but ask us to ensure it is clean and dry. So all kinds of paper, all plastics including clingfilm, metal cans and foil go all together, clean and dry, into a tough, clear plastic sack which is collected weekly at the gate at the same time as any black bagged rubbish there might be. The two sorts of bag go together into the lorry, to be separated at the depot. The crusher in the lorry does not break the tough, clear sacks, already pierced by air holes. A recycling company sorts the contents on conveyer belts.

What is left? Not much. We take glass to the bottle bank, wear-able clothes to the clothes bank. The carcass of a chicken is boiled to make stock then wrapped in newspaper and put it in the wood-burning stove where it waits till we next need a fire, once a week maybe. Cheese rind, bacon rind, scraps of fat are put out for the birds, on a feeder high above the ground and away from rats. We avoid acquiring polystyrene containers, and take plastic bags with us to the shop and use them over and over till they too must be recycled. We put out a black bag about once in two months. Because everything is clean – that's easy when you get into the routine – the bin, standing right next to the Rayburn, and taking eight weeks to fill, is never smelly. We carry out the compost bucket when it's full, but it doesn't smell either.

Finding new ways of recycling stuff and avoiding the production of rubbish is obsessive. There ought to be community compost heaps in cities for allotment gardeners and parks. I don't know a keen gardener who ever has enough compost, so why not befriend one?

The end of September, and suddenly it's colder. The bumblebees have gone. I haven't seen the swallows for a few days. Leaves are falling.

Flashback to 2005. There's still the odd day that remembers summer. Two days in Cardiff, cloudless and warm. Five o'clock. The sun is hot. It'll be over the yardarm by now, so I'm sipping a glass of chilled white wine at a pavement table outside Braz, the Millennium Centre restaurant, reflecting on the day, and watching people.

Poetry workshops in schools down the Bay. I thought I'd forgotten how to get primary school kids writing, but it worked. What they most had on their minds was the hurricane that hit New Orleans. Even where they did not mention it specifically, hurricane imagery came up in all the poems they wrote. I thought of the bumblebees' nest, and the whirling blades of the mower that topped it. Then the energy, cooperation, the optimism and life-force of the swarm as they immediately set about rebuilding their dome.

I'm waiting for David, and a book launch at seven. It's that hour between workers going home and the first evening people arriving for a book launch, a meeting, a drink, a concert, dinner. A few brisk walkers step out of the Senedd[2] and head for trains and car parks. Sight-seers in tee shirts stroll towards the bay. An outcry of seagulls over stone and water. The new debating chamber to my

9 The Welsh Assembly Building.

left, a glimpse of the shining waters of the new lagoon, the head-
land at Penarth. The sea, held back by the barrage, used to come
and go here. Under those calm waters are hidden limbs of mud
which, before the Docks became the Bay, were resculpted twice
a day by the Taff and the Ely and the huge tidal rise and fall in the
Severn estuary. I loved those flooding and draining rivers, the
mud, the half-submerged boats and buoys and shopping trolleys,
but I enjoy this gleaming surface too. Down there, I know, the
secret rivers still flow, arteries in the sea.

I remember a hot childhood day with my father when we came
to see the big ships in the dock. We walked between one dock and
another, stepping over rails and railway sleepers where the trucks
went, and just here, fluttering in the salty sea-grasses, we saw a
small blue butterfly. It flutters still, among the impressions, the
then, the now, and all that has happened in between, just here.

It feels like September in France, evening in a sunlit square in a
European city, a café table, a notebook, a glass of wine, and I'm
glad of it.

The Lineage of Bees

October

'October is marigold', as Ted Hughes reminds us, 'and yet', he continues:

> A glass half full of wine left out
>
> To the dark heaven all night, by dawn
> Has dreamed a premonition
>
> Of ice across its eye[1]

I don't need the book. I have the poem by heart. I've kept it some-where deep in memory since I first read *The Hawk in the Rain* in 1957 when I was young and ready to have my mind blown by poetry. Out there in the garden, the fields and the far hills I can see it, 'Mari-gold', all the red-golds in the spectrum with a tinge of Mary-blue like the plumage of pheasants shot and hung, the colour of deciduous decay, hallowed and haloed by the word, chilled by forewarning.

Poetry is the truth. It can warn, and foretell. 'And now it is about to start', says Hughes, fifty years before we took seriously the prospect of global warming, and, of imagining another Ice Age, 'the reunion of Mammoth and Sabre-tooth'. In the last line his words squeeze and freeze the heart before letting it go.

A poem is the only work of art you can have for nothing. Read it, memorise it, copy it into your notebook, and it's yours. It enters

9 'October Dawn'.

your mind as you sleep, like the juice of the flower love-in-idleness which Puck poured into Titania's ear as she slept. You wake up feeling different and you don't know why, until it's October again, or some other time or place or circumstance, and the right poem comes out of dream-time to meet the occasion.

October, and in between marigold days, autumn has been taking itself apart. Every dawn there is more sky, and fewer leaves.

In the first week we take the honey, thirty-seven pounds of clear amber poured from the tap of the spinner. I pass each clean jar. It's tedious, but not to be missed. I feel somehow honoured to be part of this seasonal rite of harvest. Every year the honey is different. Once, when one of our neighbours planted his field with peas to be used as cattle fodder, the honey was pale lemon and tasted smoky. This year it is a deeper gold. I can't discern its alchemy. We are quiet because David is concentrating on winding in the golden rope without losing a drop. I pass the jars and think of bees in legend and history. The white bees of the Mabinogion, the holy bees in the Laws of Hywel Dda, the tenth-century Welsh king, friend of Alfred the Great of England. I lick my fingers a lot, tonguing the honey for its complexity like a wine taster. I take a piece of honeycomb into my mouth and hold it there until I'm left with nothing but the wax. There's not much else to do when your function in life is to be a passer of jars.

David opens the tap and fills the jar, holding it steady as the stream uncoils, filling the jar to the brim. Then he turns the tap off, and with a deft flick of the jar like a waiter twisting a wine bottle to withhold its drip, he passes it to me. I hold it to the light, wipe it clean. Later we label the jars and store them in the dark. It's a hot and tiring job, working in the warm kitchen spinning the drum by hand, while the wax melts in the capping tray over hot water. There's a temptation to get cross, but I fight it. It seems important to honour this as an ancient, sacred task practised in almost every country on earth. It seems right to be calm when the bees have given all their summer for this, gathering, filling and sealing each hexagonal cell. Now we have sliced the wax cap from each comb and have spun the honey from the frames. The slices of wax go sliding down the hot capping tray like flotsam downstream. There's always some honey remaining, cells still sealed, honey left in the wax that even the centrifugal force of the spinner fails to dislodge. Wax, pollen, dust, wings and other bee detritus are caught like foam on a weir, and the last drops of honey first run then diminish to a slow dripping clean into a jug.

We work in silence. I think of bees with affection and wonder, of the single-mindedness of the swarm, as if a bee were not an individual but part of a body called the swarm, part of a mind called the swarm. Here my character, 'Story', in *Honey*, describes the moment when the bees swarm:

> Once upon a time a queen lived with her courtiers in a palace of wax. The queen is the heart and mind of the body called 'swarm'. One July day something moved inside her. Instinct surged through her. To fly, up sticks and go. To leave the palace with its many chambers and its store of gold, where the infant bees were raised in their honey scented nursery, where she feasted on nothing but royal jelly, where, once she had no use for him, every male died or was driven out and stung to death, where she has basked in opulence all her life. Despite the beauty of the hive's internal architecture, despite the intricacy of her court, despite the discipline of the swarm, she would go. She would leave everything, with no sure place to rest before nightfall, taking sixty thousand female worker bees with her. It is her duty. She must save the swarm.[2]

One of my favourites books, *Hywel Dda*, 'The Law', tells of the importance of bees in legend and in early times. Hywel Dda, a medieval King of Wales who died in about the year 950, codified the Welsh law in a marvellously poetic document of reason and humanity. It shines a lamp of insight into the dark world of the tenth century. According to the Law on Bees, translated from Welsh:

> The lineage of bees is from Paradise, and it was because of man's sin that they came from there and that God gave them his grace; and therefore the mass cannot be sung without the wax.

---

2 *Honey*, a play for radio, broadcast on BBC Radio 4, 2005.

It continues: 'The value of an old colony, twenty-four pence. The value of the first swarm, sixteen pence; the value of the bull-swarm, twelve pence.'[3] The value of the queen bee in tenth-century Wales was twenty-four pence – a great deal of money.

A bee settled on Plato's lip when he was a baby, bringing him the gift of honeyed words. According to Muhammed bees are souls. In another story the queen bee sought shelter from the storm at the door of a cruel king, and he turned her away, saying, 'Where you made your summer's honey, there make your winter quarters.'

On warm October days the bees are still out, foraging for nectar in the gorse blossom and late garden flowers. While they are in the hive, at night and on cold or wet days, the female workers spend their time keeping the space inside the palace at a perfect temperature by vibrating their million wings. If you put your ear to the hive you can hear them, a deep and distant orchestra of strings.

Flashback to October 2005. At a grand birthday luncheon for the city in the ballroom of the City Hall in Cardiff, the guests stood to sing 'Happy Birthday' to the city on the day of its centenary, 28 October. One of the last times I was in that room was at a going-down ball when I was a student. We danced to the music of John Dankworth and Cleo Laine. She was – still is – stunning. I can still feel the beat and the heat.

I had to bring a new poem to read at Cardiff's birthday party. Two days earlier I was still staring at the page, hoping I could bring off some sort of poem in time. I had an idea – I would research the architect who designed the City Hall and the Law Courts, the first two buildings on the sixty-acre park given to Cardiff by the Marquis of Bute. The architect was E.A. Rickards, a remarkable young man who went on to design Methodist Central Hall, Westminster. The story of how Rickards brought a friend by moonlight to view his two brand new, gleaming Portland stone buildings was romantic enough to set my poem going. By 1905 the City Hall and the Law Courts were complete, the finest buildings in what

3   Translated by Dafydd Jenkins (Gomer Press, 1990).

would become one of the leafiest, most generously spaced civic centres in Britain, white buildings set along wide avenues of elms – now all lost to Dutch Elm Disease, and replaced by less magnificent trees.

Each later building in the City Centre was a little less lovely, less lavish, less ample. A high moment in the new city's wealth and confidence came and went, and the buildings that completed the plan suffered from increasingly hard-nosed attitudes to how the profits of coal should be spent, despite Cardiff being the biggest coal-exporting port in the world. It was the labour of the miners which paid for those lovely buildings. While I leaned over my degree papers, scribbling, on a stifling June day in 1958, I heard the beat of drums and brass as the miners' brass bands passed down Museum Avenue. It was the annual Miners' Gala, the sound of summer. There were maybe a thousand working mines in those days in South Wales. The Thatcher government of the 1980s closed almost all of them. The drums of summer are silenced.

2006. Heatwave. Our pond is a moon-crater throughout a dry March and April. It is crazed as an earthenware bowl all of the longest, hottest, driest of all summers. October goes out like a lion. At last, in just a few days of late October downpour, the pond is alive again, full to the lip, a brimming meniscus of water.

2007. Rain, rain, rain. The pond fills to overflowing in rainy May, and is full still. A pair of mallards pause there for a few days. A heron watches the water and lifts off, trailing its legs in flight. An otter visits sometimes, upstream via the Bwdram from the Glowan. We never see it, but we know it comes.

Missing things can be as powerful as seeing them. Looking prints the mind with an imagined image. One moonlit spring night David shone his torch on the water to look for newts. There was a loud splash, and the torch showed the whole surface of the pond in turmoil and the water cloudy. Something dived in and concealed itself at the deep end, or maybe scarpered in a fright and was off along the bed of the stream too fast for even a glimpse by torchlight. Next day I took traces of prints from the muddy ground among rushes at the edge, and I found a half-eaten frog with its skull peeled. We consulted the Otter Trust, who described the skinned frog skull as a clue to typical otter behaviour, and they faxed us prints of otter and mink. Our night visitor was certainly an otter. We have never seen it, but for us it is always present, part of the pond's story, the splash, the prints, and the frog's skull clean as the moon.

The absent otter is as real as the osprey I missed at Cwmtydu. It was the last night of a course at Tŷ Newydd where I had been tutoring for the week when David phoned to tell me the news. A migrating osprey had been sighted at Cwmtydu, taking a rest on its journey from Lapland to Africa. Local people had been feeding it fish from the chip shop, and kept it a secret to protect it and to keep twitchers away. I couldn't sleep for imagining the great white bird and for longing to get home to see it. Next evening we sat on the cliffs over the sea for hours until we were frozen stiff, while the imagined osprey soared above the cliffs and the sea, its absence as haunting as a presence.

The pond contains the otter as Cwmtydu contains the osprey. They haunt the word pond, the name Cwmtydu. All words are haunted.

The skies over the October garden are swept by drifts of leaves, migrating birds and flocks of starlings. I view it all through the glass walls of this room, built onto the end of our 200-year-old long-house, making a longhouse even longer. Such a huge flock of starlings passes over a neighbour's field that they set the sheep running. They dip and swoop low over the field, a black cloud of birds, so many that I can hear them like tuning 'cellos. They take nearly a minute to pass.

As the trees undress layer by layer, leaves pile up in the porch and along the terrace. It's a job to keep up with the clearing, raking and carrying to the compost heaps, and scooping the leaves from the moat with a child's fishing net bought in a shop in New Quay. It is perfect for the job and makes fishing out leaves satisfying. The chestnut is early to leaf, early to fall. The three great beech trees on the bank on our south border each have their own timetable.

The Tir Gofal inspectors don't approve of beech in these parts. According to Tir Gofal beech is not a native species. I showed our first inspector published records of beech pollen found in Ceredigion dating from before the last Ice Age. He would not have it. Conservationists don't count time before the last Ice Age. The native species are those listed here in our time, in Britain, specifically Ceredigion since the last Ice Age. We have to stick to species that belong to the place and post-Ice-Age called the here and now. Nevertheless, beech is everywhere in the hedgerows here, common as ash, hawthorn, blackthorn and oak. Even the hornbeam, long native to south Wales, brought a frown of disapproval from that stern first inspector.

Our beautiful hornbeam avenue that rides between Cae Blaen Cwrt and Cae Bach, planted for us by John Brook to celebrate the turn of the millennium, is now about fifteen feet tall. I love the parallel stems of the trees paired west-east across the central ride, and the shadows they cast. I love it now in autumn when some of the leaves have fallen, with a ruff of brown leaves holding on all winter on the lower branches as on beech trees. I love it in snow when the shadows draw blue lines aslant the track, and in spring when the daffodils come, multiplying every year from the first hundred we planted when the trees were new. The sheep love it too. In lambing time we let in the ewes with new lambs. Shady in the heat, sheltered from wind and rain in winter, it is now a haven, hedged to the east by blackthorn, hawthorn, ash, beech, and other native hedge plants, and skirted to the west by mixed woodland, all planted at the same time. As the leaves fall, nests are revealed in the bare branches. Now there is birdsong where there was silence in the bleak, wind-swept space that preceded it.

Three big beech trees mark the boundary between our garden and Allt Maen's land, and there is something odd about their separate habits. The three trees leaf and un-leaf in sequence, the same every year, right to left, south-west to south-east, just keeping a skirt of bronze leaves about the bole all winter when the crowns are leafless. Every year the finest tree, the one to the south-east, comes into leaf three weeks later than the others, and is always the last to lose its leaves. I attributed this to their position, the direction of sunlight, the prevailing wind, until a botanist told me it indicates that the trees are not genetically related. This tells me that maybe somebody planted them, or that the seeds came with bird-droppings from a passing flock, but that they didn't seed themselves from a parent tree which might once have grown there, on the same spot.

This reminds me that I read that the reason all the elm trees of Britain died in the same short period in the last quarter of the twentieth century is that they were genetically identical. They were clones. This indicates that they were all propagated from one tree, brought by the Romans. Our beech trees are from more varied stock, and are older. They are truly native British trees, if not to Ceredigion, but they are welcome incomers anyway.

Poetry sees the month out, 'season of mists and mellow fruitfulness'. It is mild and dry, but for Keats' mists, and we bring in the last of the sweetcorn, cucumbers, beans, green tomatoes to ripen in a basket, red ones to make into tomato sauce for winter dishes. There are still bees about, murmuring over late flowers 'Until they think warm days will never cease'.

This garden is big enough for us to forget whole corners for weeks at a time. One day we check the bees in the hive at the end of the garden where John Brooks planted an ellipse of fruit trees for us about nine years ago. At almost a thousand feet above sea level we are above what gardeners call 'the fruit line', but we thought it worth a try. Marged's old garden, close to the house, had apple trees, plum trees and gooseberry bushes. Marged's apple trees were ancient and had canker and have gone; her gooseberries stood in the way of new building and garden improvements; the plums still give us many pounds of fruit every year. Of the new trees at the bottom of the garden, two apple trees produce a few small fruits; the new plum tree looks promising, then all its fruit goes mouldy. The tree closest to the hive we'd entirely forgotten about. A straggly tree, we could not remember what it was, even when, this hot April, it was covered with beautiful pink blossoms. Later, tiny fruits grew where the blossom had been – we thought it a pear tree.

So this October day we go down to the end of the garden to check the bees, and we see a wonder. The straggly, anonymous tree is lit with yellow fruit, spaced carefully as lights on a Christmas tree. The fruits are woolly to touch, and look like pears. Quince! I remember now. I had planted the tree for my mother, an unusual tree with a lovely name to remember her by when she died. Because till now it never drew attention to itself in that far corner, never bore blossom or fruit, we gradually forgot its name and provenance. I gather the fruit at once and consult Monty Don about quince jelly. I learn that the quince tree loves to paddle in wet ground. So, it was the summer of rain that brought us the miracle of the lit bush. The simmering fruit looks scummy and murky, the yellow turns a kind of khaki. I strain it, as instructed, and leave the jelly-bag to drip. Later I fill the jars with a scented rose-coloured jelly as clear and beautiful as stained glass.

The garden's done, stored in jars and freezer. As the month ends we begin to imagine winter, though still it seems warm days will never cease. The bird-silence is breaking. Apart from swallows and collared doves, the first bird to sing since July is the robin. Its small song, the first of the winter, recalls Keats' lines:

> The redbreast whistles from a garden-croft;
> And gathering swallows twitter in the skies.[4]

Sometimes these days, when the sun is on the hive, we see bees crawl from the opening to fly, but they don't go far. Soon their citadel will have the shuttered look of a chateau closed for the winter.

4 *Ode To Autumn.*

A White-Collared Blackbird

November

Darkness. Days are shortening anyway, but the sudden plunge into dark afternoons inflicted on us by the turning back of the clocks at the end of October is a shock. For a while it leaves us feeling deprived and imprisoned. Fall is a fall into darkness. All Saints. All Souls. All Hallows. All light seeps away, each day narrowing by a few more seconds in the countdown to the winter solstice.

Yet all the shortening day, from here at the table as I write, there is enough light to watch the birds: a greater spotted woodpecker brightening the show among the common crowd at the feeder; a heron, sudden and low over Allt Maen's field; a kite over the garden so close we look each other in the eye. Just now a huge flock of starlings passing over the garden, low and close, a whirring shoal that divides and merges into one again.

And the blackbird. In winter there is always a female blackbird on the forage. This year she is the distinctive bird with her necklace of white beads, white cheek freckles and a scrap of white lace on her head. She appeared last winter, nested in the hedge by the lane, raised a brood of fledglings, withdrew in July, and is now here every day. When I first saw her I feared that her strange marking might single her out as a freak and that she might be rejected by the other birds. But she is sociable, and her mate is an ordinary blackbird, black and handsome, foraging beside her in the bark mulch. I've heard it said that every blackbird has one white feather somewhere in its plumage, like a flake of snow.

I watch the beech trees too, imperceptibly changing in changing light. Time speeds up for the birds, which must feed and take in energy in shortening days. Time slows for trees. They have all the time in the world to reserve or expend their energy. To imagine their root system is awesome, as great a reach under the ground as their branches and twigs make upward and outward against the sky. An upside down tree in the dark. I can see almost the whole of each of the three beech trees framed by the glazed east wall and south gable of this room, flooded with the few hours of light that November offers. Even on a November afternoon, dusk at four thirty and getting earlier, the far fields losing definition, colour draining from the garden, there is a black and white world of sky and skeleton trees and flights of birds to see. The room is a perfect hide for bird- and weather-watching. The birds are used to it. This year November belies its reputation in literature. No fog. No cold. It has been warm and still enough in the early weeks to work in the garden in tee shirts, and no heating has been needed. We sweep the last chestnut and beech leaves from the terrace, fish them from the bottom of the moat, and mow the lawns for the last time this year. The lawnmower gathers and chews the leaves to prepare excellent leaf-mould.

A few Novembers back it rained and rained, and for the very first time, the sloping planes of the ceiling were dappled with reflections of rain dancing on floodwater, the effect we'd had in mind when we planned our 'moat'. We are all getting used to exceptional rainfall, but here in the west it used to be rare for rain to fall continuously for twenty-four hours. Our weather was always on the move, a fine morning then a wet afternoon, a rainy day with a clear sky at sunset, a wet night followed by a beautiful morning. That year, as the rain fell like a waterfall all night and all day, there was soon a most exciting flood. When the glass-walled room was built the year before, we had a trench dug outside the south and east perimeter walls. It was to be lined with water-proofing material to collect rainwater from the roof and overflow into the source of the little Bwdram in the south corner of the garden. We imagined our moat stirred by the least wind, the ceiling a shimmer of water-light. We dreamed of stepping out on summer evenings through the two pairs of French windows across sandstone slab bridges over the water between the house and the to-be-built terrace. The moat lay unfinished and unlined, the terrace unlaid. That winter it was just a trench, without overflow, between the walls and the grass. Just a clay trench. Water tires of waiting. Water knows its place. It has a will of its own and will find its level, so after months of dry weather, for the first time since we built the room we had our moat. As the rain threatened never to stop, and as there was no way to channel it harmlessly away, David fetched the long hose from the shed and siphoned the flood-water across the terrace-to-be and over the garden into the stream. The hose dipped and rose in the trench, sipping and gulping like a yellow water serpent, and the water level went down, down.

Now the sandstone terraces to the east and south, the low sand-stone walls whose stones were mostly gathered from the land, the moat and its two bridges, are completed. Rain in any season is now a pleasure. It tap-dances the terrace and gushes from the new gutters turning the surface to ripples. When the moat is full to an inch of the brim, the water takes to the overflow to augment the stream, risen to new importance as a water course.

The 'stream' is usually not much more than a winterbourne, rising from the spring in the corner of the garden where the Bwdram is born, giving the house part of its name, *blaen*, source. Normally a trickle, at times like that torrential November, and in the recent wettest summer ever recorded, the tiny Bwdram came into its own, rushing down hill to the pond, to the valley, to join the Glowan, the Clettŵr, the Teifi, the Irish Sea. Water has moments of importance as well as moments of reflection.

So to this November which begins warm and dry, allowing the glass doors to open on stillness, the garden the colours of Eastern rugs – old rose, terracotta, amber and ochre, a low sun picking gold from the fallen skirt of leaves round acer and beech. It could be late summer, but for the lost hour of daylight, darkness hastened even more by shortening days.

The feeders have been busy for weeks. Tits, finches, wrens, robins, willow warblers, the woodpecker. One starling comes for easy pickings from the peanut feeder, leaving its flock grazing the field over the hedge. The small birds do not like the starling. The white-feathered blackbird is here with her mate, a little woman out shopping, picking in the leaf-piles under bushes, saying nothing. Siani, the border collie, conscientious about her calling, sees off the magpies. She lies quietly, one gold eyebrow raised, one amber eye alert, while the blackbirds pick close to her, but when the magpies appear she is driven to madness, barking hopelessly into the trees.

Weather and birds and journeys and people. A few Novembers ago the North Atlantic Oscillation made the weather forecasters very excited. They talked of a hard and snowy winter, a winter out of legend, like '47, '64, '82. We were overdue for one, they said. The North Atlantic Oscillation, that oceanic dance of wind and waves and deep, deep currents, was coming up for a roll again. I try to understand it. As the planet tilts, the Gulf Stream is carried a little further north into the Atlantic, Greenland warms a little, and northern Scandinavia gets colder. We have weaker westerly winds from the Atlantic, anti-cyclones settle in the North Sea, and the snows begin to fall. The stalling of an anti-cyclone in the North Sea is kind to Wales. Protected from the worst of the blizzards by the hinterland and the mountains, kept temperate as usual by the sea, we relish the rare treat of a long spell of cold, clear, dry weather, with just enough snow to slow the world without causing misery. We dreamed of watching snow fall through the glass walls of our warm room, of snowy walks in a luminous and purified world. Dream on. The legendary winter did not happen.

Journeys. On the train out of Aberystwyth, on my way to Durham for a reading, I meet a blind musician. I am keeping my head down on the crowded little train, avoiding involvement with a family on an outing. They are scattered before and behind me, shouting to each other across the aisle and the backs of their seats. I don't dare catch the eye of the baby in case it encourages the shouting grandmother to bring me into their story. I feign curmudgeonliness. From my back-to-the-engine seat, I listen to the blind man in his face-the-engine seat on the other side of the aisle, engage the young mother in conversation. He has the voice and accent of an ex-public school boy. He begins: 'How old is the baby?' 'Boy or girl?' An only child?' 'Wasn't the bomb attack in London terrible? Will we get bombed, do you think?' The very young mother, tattooed and body-pierced, answers every question graciously. I am relieved I don't have to talk. The mother leaves her seat for a moment, and the man speaks. 'Where are we?' he says, to no one. 'Is that the ticket collector?' What can I do but reply? I promise to

tell him when the train manager passes our way. He at once
discovers where I am going and why, my occupation, my name,
and that I've had books published. I soon know he is a pianist on
his way to a conference in Bognor Regis, a week of performing
music with other blind musicians, and that he is due to play a piece
by Beethoven which is usually played much too fast. 'Terrible
about that bomb,' he says. 'And all the train crashes. Are we safe
on this train?' I assure him we could not be safer, that we are trav-
elling on a single-track line, that the little train would pause close
to Caersws to wait for the down train, and that it would not
continue its journey until the down train has passed us, and the
two drivers have exchanged a token. (I'm not sure what they do,
but it works.) The train gives a little cry, a shout of joy, as it
approaches each unmarked crossing, farm track and country lane
in the back of beyond. He is like a child asking, 'Are we nearly
there?' He is in my charge now. It's up to me to talk to him, stow
his case in the gap behind my seat and guide his hand to it, to stop
the train manager for him and to name all the stations. Then, the
announcement. 'This train will not proceed to Birmingham New
Street. All alight at Wolverhampton and take the next train to New
Street.' This sabotages my journey – I am sure to miss my tight
connection at New Street. But for the blind man it is a disaster.
His pre-arranged assistance will not be there. Two unaided
changes of train lie ahead.

At Wolverhampton I place him in the hands of the station
manager. Assistance, called Alex, comes loping down the steps two
at a time, and places an arm under the blind man's elbow. They
step out like a couple. The blind musician and I catch the same
overcrowded train out of Wolverhampton. I notice it is due to call
at Watford Junction, his connecting station for Bognor Regis. I
tell him not to change at Birmingham, but to stay put for Watford.
The train is packed, and I stow his case close to his seat and settle
him beside a young Asian. 'Are you English?' he asks his new
neighbour. 'Yes,' says the Asian. The young man and I grin at each
other. I know the blind man will ask if the train is safe, and that
the young Asian will reassure him. He's a white-feathered black-
bird but he doesn't know it.

I think about a life in darkness, the blessing that he, with his
posh English accent, and perhaps the prejudices of his class and

generation, is able to talk easily and without preconception to a tattooed teenage mother, a travelling bard, a young Muslim man. I think of the curse of living in fear of what he can't see or guess at. Is it worse than a life in silence? Bees are deaf. They can see. They can smell. They build exquisite palaces from the secretions of their own bodies, and control its temperature with the vibrations of their wings. They can't hear the 'cello music of their wings, or of Beethoven. I miss my connection for Durham at Birmingham New Street.

Before we know it the Advent calendar will be opening its doors one by one. My main winter journeys begin. We will have performed for Poetry Live in thirteen cities by Christmas.

After a companionable 25-mile drive to the station with David, the train carries me out of Aberystwyth on a darkening Sunday afternoon, heading for Newcastle. I feel that particular sorrow associated with waving goodbye from a train that is out of all proportion with the mere five days I'll be away from home. It must be all those old films. I settle, shoring myself against the onset of homesickness with small possessions, making a private cell out of the tiny space comprising two cramped seats in the little Arriva train. David Jones describes the soldiers in France in the First World War making corners in old barns, their own nail to hang something on, their own pillow of straw. For me it's a book, phone, notebook, journal, sandwiches, bottle of Blaen Cwrt water. (You can't buy it. It rises from an aquifer fifty-four feet below our garden.) I choose the aisle seat, the one in front of the void between seatbacks where I stow my travel bag. The window seat to my right is the least likely to attract a fellow traveller. The table seats fill first, and only if the train is packed will someone ask me: 'Is anyone sitting there?' Sunset. The mountains are black on a red sky. The curve of the river and the mountain tarns are blood. A pair of kites flicker in the last light of the sun. Snow lies un-thawed in deep ravines. Aberdyfi glows, luminous across the Dyfi estuary. The sheep run as we chug up the valley out of Machynlleth, turning east into the shadows.

The train cries along the single track through steep oak woods and past lonely white farms you can't imagine ever finding by road, soon to surrender to the long winter night. The train cries through the cutting. It's a sorrowful sound. The carriage is now bright, the windows black. We have lost the great exterior to the night in exchange for this small, lit space. My mood of overwhelming melancholy will deepen until we reach the Midlands, to be swept aside by the business of changing trains at Birmingham New Street, and to lift utterly as we purr, rocking and clicking over the Tyne to arrive in Newcastle, and I'm in a taxi talking to a Geordie driver, with the prospect of the hotel, a meal, a glass of wine, a warm room, a long, hot bath. Then, five cities later, five days and evenings in the good company of poets, I'll be on my way home, going over the pleasures of the week, the liveliness of each audi-torium packed with perhaps 2,000 teenagers, the atmosphere described by a journalist as 'barely contained anarchy' that turns to silent listening as the poets step forward to the microphone to read. By mid-February, after eight weeks of touring Britain, we will have performed for 75,000 GCSE students.

30 November again. A stormy night is followed by a bright morning, puddles of sky on the terrace are creased silk in the wind. The slate table is floating with skywater like one of those brimful swimming pools that touch infinity. I have a whole day at home. We've brought in the pots of winter cactus and oxalis from their summer holiday on the terrace. They drip-dry on newspaper. They are all in flower already.

Ah! There she goes, my winter companion, life-force, *Turdus merula*, *aderyn du*, *mwyalchen*, *iâr*, little brown hen of the garden with her dusting of snow-feathers, foraging in the mulch. I love her for her ordinariness, her lineage linking her to the earliest Welsh and Irish poetry and to the monks in their scriptoria. I look forward to an end of the seven months of bird silence, to her glossy black mate's first dawn aria from the crown of a beech tree. They make me believe in the future again.

Water like a Stone

December

Keats sends me a t-mail (time-mail, not invented at the time of writing, but it's bound to happen):

> Saint Agnes Eve, ah bitter chill it was,
> the hare limp'd trembling through the frozen grass ...
> the owl for all his feathers was a-cold.

Christina Rossetti takes up the theme:

> In the bleak midwinter
>   Frosty wind made moan,
> Earth stood hard as iron,
>   Water like a stone,
> Snow had fallen, snow on snow,
>   Snow on snow,
> In the bleak midwinter
>   Long ago.[1]

The resonance of 'long ago', such an ordinary phrase, a cliché even, touched me for the first time at a Christmas concert in Talgarreg village primary school in December 1995. Our three oldest grandchildren had spent the summer holidays with us. By September, back from completing a two-year postgraduate degree course in Newcastle, my daughter was still house-hunting in Cardiff, so the children stayed on with us as the winter term began, and we sent

---

1   Keats, 'The Eve of St Agnes'; Christina Rossetti, 'A Christmas Carol'.

them to the Welsh-language village school. They lost their briefly acquired Geordie accents, and became Welsh children.

At the concert the children sang carols, recited, performed little dramas and a Nativity scene, all in Welsh. Then Cai took the stage and recited Christina Rossetti's poem in English. Outside it was cold. There was no snow, but earth stood hard as iron, and the water in our pond was 'like a stone'. Cai spoke clearly and plainly. Freed from the familiar (and beautiful) tune the words became a poem again. Its ice-sharp language spoke a poem's truth, crisp with monosyllabic words, the five longer words – midwinter, frosty, water, fallen, ago – simple cadences like phrases of birdsong among the monosyllables that skittered across the icy night. Cai's teacher that term was a distinguished, published Welsh poet, a chaired bard who well understood a poem's value in either language. I held my breath. Cai, my ten-year-old grandson, was speaking a great poem. I had never heard it spoken before, though I'd sung it countless times as a carol. Cai, well-rehearsed by his teacher, did not falter. 'Long ago,' he said slowly, 'Long ago'.

Centuries slipped from the history book. I imagined that 'long ago', before cars, before electricity, before tarmac, the roads mud-tracks, the cottages thatched, in this village perhaps, or anywhere, the snows falling in every 'long ago' as far back in time as the poem could take us. I gazed through poetry's windows into the past, verse beyond verse, stanza on stanza, sonnet beyond sonnet, *englynion* opening into each other, farther and deeper. I was a passer-by in the street who stops to look in through a window at a bright room, inhabited but soundless, the glass of silence like time between us. I thought of Larkin's 'snow fell undated', and shivered. Language was new again that night, simple language with no theatricals, no showy poetics, just the spell that a poem is, the innocence of a school Christmas concert. The plain truth of it.

Fast forward ten Decembers. 2005. Poetry Live gigs over for the Christmas break, I have poems to write and visits to and duties for Cardiff. The October hundredth-birthday lunch is followed by a grand dinner to celebrate the fiftieth anniversary of the day Cardiff was declared the Capital of Wales, on the eve of the winter solstice.

A new poem wanted, with one week's notice! I well remember the declaration fifty years ago. In school we took sides: Cardiff v. Swansea. For me there was no contest. How could my city of superlatives not be the obvious choice? The biggest coal exporting port in the world; the loveliest city centre, with more green spaces than any; the most diverse ethnic population, the oldest established immigrant community; the second highest rise and fall of the tide in the world. Already, as a child, I was in thrall to the white buildings in their avenues and lawns, and was a familiar in the Natural History galleries of the museum. But what clinched it for me were the stone animals on the castle wall. Especially the bear. The bear and I voted for Cardiff.

I try to ignore Christmas. It all starts too soon. I hate the bling, the cheap glitter, the unremitting materialism, the waste, the flashing lights, the destruction of rural darkness by the spreading disease of giant illuminated nodding Santas and snowmen and, God help us, flashing inflatable cribs. I want an airgun for Christmas so that I can shoot Santa Claus and watch him deflate with a hiss. Lights fidget on houses all the way from Ceredigion to Cardiff, eating the ozone layer and melting the Greenland glaciers. Where is the romance of the one lit tree in the window we used to count on winter walks with the kids? Bah! Humbug!

I have a theme for the Cardiff poem, but they won't like it. The winter solstice. The darkest night. The year's midnight. We brazen out the narrowing days with light. Out there in the temperate city an ice rink glitters on a civic lawn as if we dreamed Victorian glitter when lakes were dancing floors, the rivers froze for goose fairs and all was marble winter. For now, the city puts on party clothes. We say, dress every tree with electricity. Switch on the lights. Let streets and houses glow. When the party's over, and we step into the night and feel the Ice Queen's wand of cold, an imagined hush of snow will touch the heart, and we'll know that for the pleasures of here and now we are borrowing bling from the glacier, slipping Greenland's shoulder from its wrap of snow.

Oh, ice-makers, who can make a frozen floor

in the maritime air of our mild city,
bring your alchemy to the melting permafrost.

Chain the glacier. Put the wilderness under locks.
Rebuild the gates of ice. Hold back the melt-water
for footfall of polar bear and Arctic fox.[2]

Fast forward again to the now of a cold, dry December. Frost glitters on the sandstone terrace, and on the hedge banks frost stays white all day. The slate table is laid with glitter. I put a red enamel plate of crumbs on its cloth-of-silver for the robins, who do not like the bird feeder. The birds are getting through all the seed, nuts, crumbs, bacon fat, cheese rind I can give them – sacks of it. There are treecreepers in the plum trees, a greater spotted woodpecker on the nut holder. The white-collared female blackbird sees off two male competitors for food – or is she displaying her spirit and resourcefulness, ready for spring mating?

We walk hard-frozen ground to check and count the sheep. One year, before Christmas we lost a yearling ram. Accurately counting sheep can be difficult. The little ram may have got under a gate. By the time we found him he had been alone for weeks. He was thin and weak, found wandering at the far end of the wood where no sheep ought to have been. We brought him home, fed him, gave him shelter for a few days, and he improved. We kept him in the field closest to the house, and watched him grazing there, thinking he'd make it. But sheep are strange animals. They don't thrive on their own. They are flock creatures and seem to lose the will to live when away from their kind. One day we could not see him grazing in the field. He had found a corner to die in. The wool torn from his fleece by the crows lay scattered on the grass for months. It was later taken by nesting birds. Nothing goes to waste in nature. That winter our Christmas cards used his story, and a photograph of our midsummer hayfield. The poem expected him to live. The words celebrate his response to us, the slow improvement in his strength, and the good sight of him pulling clean hay from the manger. By Christmas he had changed his mind and lost heart, and one night he lay down in the field to die. Such

2 'Solstice' (unpublished).

failures always hurt. As children we learn the pain of the loss of animals: guinea pigs, hamsters, birds saved from the jaws of a cat. But it still hurts.

On Christmas Eve, we bring in the tree – a blue spruce – and while David is off over the land gathering greenery to deck the hall – our glass-walled dining room – I listen to the Festival of Nine Lessons and Carols on the radio, and unpack the box of decorations. I take them out one by one and hang them on the tree, yet again remembering each one from somewhere, or someone. A few are so old they date from my own childhood, many from the time when the children were little. Will I always do this? Would I do it if I lived alone? In 1984, before electricity, before a bathroom, towards the end of my first term as Poet in Residence at Lampeter, during my one winter living alone here at Blaen Cwrt, I hung a real but tiny tree with papier mâché apples and simple stars cut from white paper. It was just for me. Then David arrived from Aberystwyth and we drove home to Cardiff to a proper house with electricity for Christmas with the family, and we dressed a proper tree with the contents of that old Christmas box.

Unpacking the Angel

Twelve papier mâché apples.
Eleven glass balls, one broken.
My children swim to me from their brittle windows.
Birds from the mirrors in the rich lady's house
when Dylan was three, and beautiful.

Tangled strands of Woolworths' lametta,
saved nearly forty years from a first flat.
Putti from Venice, from Bellini and Canaletto,
from the flaking plaster of churches,
They feather the room like light off water.

The journey to Bethlehem in brass.
The crib from Tübingen. The Holy Family

I made from Polyfilla, wire and rags.
Snarled strings of light bulbs on green flex,
vines of stars, the lights of far-off cities.

Two crystal drops from the fair on the Kurfürstendamm,
rousing from the drafts that stir the tree
the whine of air-raids, a church in flames, stained glass bursting.
And the Berlin angel whose sleeves still bear
a trace of concrete from the broken wall.

On the twelfth day we'll undress the tree:
twelve papier mâché apples, eleven balls,
ten birds, lametta, putti, painted crib,
the Holy Family, the burning city,
angels of mercy and death.

All into the box with flakes
of human skin, glitter, glass,
pine-needles sifted to corners,
and under the flaps, dust, maybe,
from every year of my life.[3]

These days we stay home for Christmas, just the two of us, leaving
time before and after for family visits. I remember the tense family
Christmases of childhood, the house full of aunts, steam, wrapping
paper, fripperies and disappointment, my mother run off her feet,
and it all ending in tears. Then lovely Christmases in our house in
Cardiff when the children were young, with a few extra family
members, games, a concert and without television. This house is
too small to accommodate the whole family, so we hunker down
for the festival, the two of us, dog, cats, and spend the day our way.
We check the sheep, have a picnic lunch, come home in the dark-
ening afternoon to read, sip and listen to music in a house rich with
the juices of a slowly roasting goose.

But it is still Christmas Eve. David returns, laden with larch
boughs, holly and ivy from the wood. He begins his annual task

3 *Five Fields* (Carcanet, 1998).

of dressing the room. I have finished the tree and switch on the lights. It's almost dark outside, and the tree is reflected in every sheet of glass, a twinkling forest. Scents rise in the warmth. Spruce needles. Spices. Twigs of witchhazel from the garden shaking out perfumed yellow petals. David lays his branches along the walls between the glass and the eaves, and he selects especially elegant, long larch sprays for the lateral steel stays that tie the room's oak frame. Then I pass him my favourite angel, a lute player with porcelain face, hands and feet, in flight in her stiffened gold robes like an angel in a Renaissance painting. She will fly for twelve days, and then return to her cell, a cardboard box, for the rest of the year. For the time being I can believe in it all again.

Once upon a time there is a white Christmas. The tree and room are decked, the feast prepared, my presents for David wrapped and placed under the tree. It is nearly midnight on Christmas Eve. I look up at the Velux window over the kitchen and see snow falling. It falls all night, and by morning the fields are laid with fresh linen. All is silent and dazzling. On Christmas morning we open our 'stockings' (David's thick red walking-boot socks) packed with things for the five senses, and always a book. We leave the bird to roast slowly for our evening dinner, take a picnic and binoculars and walk the land. David has checked the sheep and filled the racks with hay. We can see for miles, white mountains folding beyond each other to the high, far peaks of Cader Idris and Snowdon across the curve of Cardigan Bay. We walk in the new snow and sit in the sun on the bank at the edge of the oak wood to have our picnic – sandwiches, a satsuma from the toe of each sock, a flask of tea. Overhead a jet gleams, leaving the wake of its passage on the sky. Its long snout noses towards the Atlantic, and America. Who on earth flies anywhere on Christmas Day? Kings and wise men, I suppose. The sheep look grubby against the dazzle of the snow, dirty as a *clwt* that wants a good bleaching. Home just as it's getting dark, to set the room sparkling, to sit reading a new book, and sip a glass of something mellow and deep red with beaded bubbles winking at the brim, while the goose 'rests' on the Rayburn, potatoes roast themselves in their herbs, plates warm, and we have only to check all those messages on the answerphone asking where we are, and phone the family, before setting our feast on the table.

Shepherd

Christmas, and over the snow
a jet chases the day,
cresting the sill of the land
to take the Atlantic.

In the fields
a man and his dog
check the sheep dawn and dusk
as they've always done.

What's it to him,
the flight of kings,
but to remind him
that the world turns,

that going home is a prayer,
that even war draws breath.[4]

On the last day of December a young neighbour calls, son of Pant Bach, as he does every year, to let us know that the Vale of Clettŵr hunt will be out drag-hunting on New Year's Day. He has taken over this task from his brother, who died tragically a few years ago. He knows, as do all members of the hunt, that we do not support hunting with dogs. He comes into the kitchen and we talk. It's nice to see him, though we know why he is here. The conversation is in Welsh. We repeat the usual rules: if the hounds cross our land, no rider must follow; if the hounds pick up the scent of a real fox, no terriers, no terrier men, no digging. As always this is courteously agreed. Some years ago, Evan from the Allt Maen family used to call. Once, as if proffering an explanation, he spoke about the *miwsig*, the music, the baying of the hounds and the sound of the huntsman's horn, 'Mae'r pobl yn hoffi'r miwsig,' he said. 'The people love the music of it.'[5]

---

4 Gillian Clarke, from *Making the Beds for the Dead* (Carcanet, 2004).
5 *Miwsig*, borrowed from English, rather than *cerddoriaeth*, is often used in speech.